The
Value
Message

The Value Message

Celebrate Your Value, Uncover Your Gift and Potential

Rolland Sarver

Dedication.

This book is dedicated to your empowerment! Whoever and wherever you are! To the person searching for a shred of hope that they must have at least some value and worth. LET THERE BE NO DOUBT!

Acknowledgments

Inspiration for this book has come from many sources. Most of whom had no knowledge at all of their significant influence through the years. Family and friends gifted me with their ear and patience, their feedback and conversation. Strangers gifted me with a smile and connection or with a story longing to be told. Thanks to all of you for your messages of hope and beacons of light.

Preface

Motivational and inspirational content are captivating to me. I eat this stuff up, podcasts, books and videos. It's my passion and interest. I'm a voracious consumer of this subject matter.

This book came as a surprise to me. In my wildest dreams (and I've had some wild ones) I never thought of writing a book, ever. Reading has always been a favorite pastime, a calming outlet. Writing a book was always someone else's project and passion. I'm your average *Joe*, not at all how I, or you picture a writer, I promise.

People have always interested me, and our many differences intrigue me. Our similarities are equally intriguing. Just being curious about what makes us tick has prompted me to search and read a lot about *what makes us tick*.

This book is about your real value and self-worth. It's about your gift and potential. It's about courage and resilience. It's about mental health and mindset. It's about hope for your present and future, freedom from your past.

A favorite story theme of mine is when the weary slave is set free. Any book or movie with this theme and I'm hooked already! Metaphorically we all have been a slave to something and know the relief of being set free.

"Fetters and chains lose their *grip,* falling *powerless* to the ground,
Setting free the weary captive once so tightly bound!"
-Anonymous

Harriet Tubman, an icon of courage and freedom, for example, inspires and stirs my emotions. I'm on the edge of my seat listening to her riveting story. The journey from fear and oppression to hope and real freedom. I cry long before the account is over. It's my genre, it's where I belong.

Some months back the thought came to me about writing

a book. It felt like the *why was* clear, but the *what* hadn't shown up yet. Neither had the title or content.

Whenever I had spare time, I started writing. I wrote when I couldn't sleep at night or when injustice was served. I wrote when people's hearts were broken. I wrote when people were overjoyed. As I became more focused on a message about value and worth, content just started to show up on the page. Technology was also on my side, you can jot down a thought or note, anywhere, anytime on your phone, tablet or computer, it's all piped into the same document. Like a puppy, it follows you wherever you go!

There must be a ton of authors on the planet because so many are ready to share their knowledge and experience in this field, for which I'm grateful. It's a friendly community. I'm still surprised every day that I'm writing a book. It's intimidating and invigorating at the same time.

The journey of my book project looks something like this; At first, "Could I write a book"? Then, "I could write a book". After a while, "I must write a book". Finally, "I am writing a book"! Why? Because someone needs to hear a message about their worth and value today and the next day, and the next day!

Table of Contents

Chapter 1. Why such a book?

A message about your value.

The validation of your value and self-worth is a message that needs to be heard and spoken loudly! I want to bring keen awareness to your innate value.

If you see your own value, will it change the world? Will understanding the truth about your value change other people? Likely not. Awareness of your own value will change the truth about *your* world, I promise! Why *not* such a book?

Statistics about self-harm, abuse, despair, loneliness and hate are an alarming message. Furthermore, effective coping skills, life skills, communication and relationships skills are in short supply. Few if any are born with such expertise. Yet we needn't be distressed by this unhealthy news report.

Many of us look for a magic pill to heal our woes. *Cure all* potions don't exist. Yet this truth doesn't keep us from searching for it. Our hurt and woes may look like those *alarming statistics*. Who wouldn't seek relief from these perilous stressors?

What could improve your entire outlook and confidence level? Getting a better grasp of your own value will significantly move the dial. You are advantaged if others see your value, you are unshakable if you see your own value and worth!

Become acutely aware of how culture, society and your own mind sees and undermines your value. You are not broken. Consider the messages daily fed to you regarding your worth. These *Value Messages,* good or bad, are tremendously impactful. Messages about value and self-worth have the power of life and death. Please, realize your marvelous worth!

A key objective of this book is to answer the following questions.

1. Why is understanding your value so important?
2. How will this be helpful to you?
3. Where is a good place to start for making a permanent change?

Who are you?

I'm curious about who you are and where you are on your journey. Is your journey one of health and learning, of growth? Do you question this cultural message; *you are only valuable if you have something I need?* Do you find yourself doing crazy things to be accepted by other people or yourself? Do you feel empty inside no matter how much of anything you consume? Are you afraid someone will expose this emptiness? Do you feel like your value has *tanked out* with little chance of being filled up? Are you grasping for any hope, any sign that your value and self-worth might be real or true? Sheesh, enough questions already, can we just move on?

If you have the option of spare time, these questions might rumble around in your mind. Many people don't have the time to think about or even imagine a different, better path. Sadly, struggling to get through the day is the plight of much of our civilization, surviving but not thriving.

Welcome to *The Circus of Life.* Under the *Big Top* are spectators, leaders, followers, clowns, performers and a host of other characters. Yes, all are playing a part in the show we call *living.*

Perhaps you are on solid ground about your worth. Hopefully, you find a *take-away* in this book. Something amazing happens when your value and worth become clear. Something inside comes to life! Scarcely tangible, but for sure has a heartbeat. It can be faintly sensed with the eye. It can be felt with the heart. It's like spiritual growth, unseen as a seed, but visible at its emergence. It's feeling like something is about to happen. Like a Monarch chrysalis beginning to move, as a beautiful new creature awakens!

Who am I?

The stories I share here aren't different from what you would share. Life brings us experiences, and we learn from them. It's like we're all on the Oregon Trail and our stories are the lessons we get while trudging along the pathway. Everyone's viewpoint is different, yet educational. The drivers, the men, the women, the children, the dogs and horses all have a different perspective of the same journey. *Mark Twain* says this about experience being the best teacher. "When you grab a bull by the tail, you will know a lot more in the end than you did in the beginning."

I can remember when the internet was born! Telling my age here. Technology has certainly altered the cultural landscape for the entire world. Last night my nine-year-old daughter, explaining technology to her younger sibling said, "We have a lot more telephone poles now, so that tells us we have more technology nowadays"!

High speed internet used to be dialed up on the phone line. Data came over the phone line, along with some obnoxious squeaking and beeping noise. You never saw slow until you've waited ten agonizing minutes for a one-megabyte picture to download. Upload was much slower. Internet service was paid for by the hour or minute. AOL (America On Line) made the most ridiculous claim you ever heard. We all laughed. They claimed soon their customers would be getting internet service 24/7. You mean you could connect to the internet all day? Didn't have to disconnect the phone line, just to connect? "Well, Larry, you know that'll never happen." Besides, why would you even need the internet when you're sleeping? There ought to be a law against companies making such empty promises!

West-central Illinois is my home. Where everyone except us has a funny accent and our way of thinking is the *most best* (kidding of course). People are shaped and influenced by their culture and environment, me included. Like you, my world view, filters and opinions are largely a result of my upbringing. Grandpa loved his Craftsman tools and carbide saw blades which, for him, revolutionized his carpentry trade. As a child I didn't know what carbide was, but I knew it was the best thing since sliced bread and the word *carbide* should be used often just to sound knowledgeable about something.

No matter the environment we are born into, we're riding someone else's *magic carpet*. In some ways every person and generation have to *reinvent the wheel* of personal and spiritual growth. At some point our own internal guidance system must come online. Then we will know where to go, not solely directed by the gift and inspiration of family or other travelers. Directed by our own *internal sense* that keeps us on the pathway.

Monarch Butterflies have a *four-generation life cycle* each year. The fourth generation have an *inborn guidance system* directing them to fly more than 2,000 miles and hibernate for the winter. This guidance system then directs them to fly north at exactly the right time, find a mate and initiate the first generation of the next year's *crop*. This phenomenon is accomplished in the absence of any *external* influence. No map, no directions, no instructions, no one to follow and having never been to the place they are going. Truly pilgrims, these spectacular creatures individually are marching to the beat of a *different drummer*! Yet individually are marching to the same destination. Not one of them is aware of the miraculous inner work that gathers them together. Have you ever watched the movie: August Rush? You can't miss the *internal guidance* theme here!

The Smart Scale

Let me explain the *Smart Scale*. This scale is a quick self-assessment of our *brain power,* relatively speaking! Albert Einstein is on the right side. Your average North American raccoon is on the left. Raccoons are soooo cute and have amazing dexterity with their paws but can't figure out how to cross the road. I'm somewhere between the raccoon on the left and the middle. Notice there's a lot of *white space* between me and Einstein!

More and more I believe what's inside all of us is the same, and yes, *you* can do extraordinary things. From this book I want you to hear and believe a message about your value. I want you to know, without a doubt you can do hard things. Great things, smart things, not so smart things, amazing things and so on. But it will have to be *you*! No matter how much we wish it were different, if your car is to get out of the garage, you alone must be the driver. Oh, and don't forget to open the garage door. Don't be afraid to open the door! To not open the door on the way out, is called self-sabotage. Dangers and wonders are in this world to be discovered, but you will never find them while parked in the garage!

"When things change inside you, things change around you." - *Unknown*

Busy Bees

Life is so busy either by accident or on purpose. Busyness can stunt your growth and creativity. Why? Because busyness gives us tunnel vision and prevents us from being aware of our self and surroundings. Busyness can have an appearance of ambition and accomplishment but leave us in the *Thick of Thin Things!*

For example, think about just taking a day off to do nothing. Who would do this? Do you get short of breath and inundated with guilt just thinking about such inaction? What would the neighbors think? Or your boss or spouse or even yourself? Does your chest feel tight at the thought of not ever getting that time back? I'm not talking about a day to work on your *to-do list*. The to-do list will always be there. Just a daytime fantasy where you sit on the back deck, drink sweet tea and feel the sunshine. No worries and no... well at least keep a robe handy in case the neighbor walks by. Give yourself permission for some rest and restoration.

Having too many *irons in the fire* has been a trend for decades. We all have different reasons for running around like chickens with our heads cut off.

1. To distract us away from facing reality.
2. So the neighbors don't think we're lazy.
3. It's just what everyone does, so I'm going to do it too.

There must be a good reason to be exhausted all the time. Why would so many people be overwhelmed with busyness if there wasn't something to it?

I must ask, "What about the time you can't get back because you spent a whole day being busy but didn't grow or learn?" Did you ever feel this way about homework as a kid? You spent many an hour on this *busywork.* Not all of it helped you learn and grow. There's something to be said for family time, leisure time, time to explore and your own time.

Some people are afraid of free time. It's not productive. Will I have any value if I'm not busy? This country will fall apart if everyone has too much free time. I say this because it's how I felt

6

at one time. Free time scares us because we can't control or see it. I can see a hammer swinging or a road getting built. I'm uneasy when I see people doing nothing. Are you saying I am a control freak?

No question that free time can be abused. Haven't I been guilty of such a thing? Yep. Deeper things can also result from free time. Learning from a book. Learning from a walk in the woods or a conversation with a friend or a stranger.

"Save us from the emptiness of a busy life." I heard these words years ago. It's a noble cause to be organized, get things done, and plan for your future. However, if your efforts are to impress the neighbors, or you are chasing a trend, you might want to rethink your motives.

Let awareness do its thing!

Once you become aware of something it's difficult or impossible to *unsee* whatever it is you just saw. Your mind explodes with curiosity, becomes anxious and suspenseful about whatever you just became aware of. Like compound interest, let awareness work for you, every day and night! Holidays and weekends too. As awareness grows, so will knowledge and education. Embrace learning new things, no matter what they are. What we know and understand is our comfort zone. Don't stay there just to avoid becoming aware of what you don't want to be aware of. The only good thing to come out of your comfort zone is you. It's called personal growth.

Be aware of being aware! Someone told me scents, like perfume, body wash and candles all come from four basic ingredients. These four *flavors* are just mixed in various amounts to create the desired outcome.

1. Woodsy
2. Musk
3. Fruity
4. Spice

When you become aware of this, moving forward, your brain will often filter the amounts of each *flavor* in any man-made scent passing through your schnoz!

Your brain is always wanting something to do. This is why you wake up at two o'clock in the morning thinking, "What's the little thing that hangs down in the back of your throat called". Or asking, "Do we all live in a yellow submarine?" Does anyone wake up at the same exact time every night? 3:36 a.m. was my time. For a number of years, I'd wake up at this time every single night, look at the clock and go back to sleep. Never did know what I was supposed to be doing or thinking. Just saying, our brains think of the craziest stuff in the middle of the night, just because it's looking for something to do. Then you know what happens when the alarm goes off? Now all your brain wants to do is go to sleep. So, now your brain has a task to focus on. Sorting out which four scents were used in the perfume you just got a whiff of. Your next visit to Bath & Body Works will be more interesting! Point being, once you become aware of this information, you can never become not aware.

When you do become more aware of your surroundings in the world, become aware of how you value yourself and others. Be an observer and a listener. Listen to the messages culture and society are giving about value. Become aware of what your ears and heart listen to.

"When our awareness awakens, it will never go back to sleep!"
-Anonymous

The objective of this book is to keep pushing your *awareness button*. Not like a fire alarm that jolts you awake or makes you pee your pants. The button push is like a notification sound on your phone, a *shoulder tap* to get your attention.

Put those two boxes on the table, please!

Can you see visionary people? Can you pick them out of a crowd? We know visionaries when what they were visualizing materializes. These people are sometimes thought of as borderline insane until what they have been talking about for years actually happens.

Jeff Bezos (is a great study, Amazon's Executive

Chairman) somewhere around the year 2000 when Amazon was mostly selling books, he had a vision. Not everyone had a computer in the living room. Cell phones were simple and basic. He rambled on about how some day everyone would have a computer and order lots of stuff right from their house or phone. He claimed the general public could order products and get them delivered the next day.

Mr. Bezos' financial and business partners were pressuring him to get a life and couldn't see what he was seeing. Didn't slow him down much, he had a vision and could see some big changes far off in the future. What an excellent time to buy Amazon stock, selling at $46. Closing stock price today is lower than it's been for a long time, $3,281 per share. If you'd bought one hundred shares, today even your wife would think you made a smart decision! Yep, if you can visualize something it may confuse your friends, but don't be discouraged. Keep a steady eye on the future.

I don't think of myself as a visionary, but I relate to visualizations and what they can do for you. Visionaries and visualizations both use the *mind's eye* to explore and create.

Let me take you on a guided visualization. Unless you are driving, take the time to close your eyes and visualize! Or at least relax, it's hard to read and close your eyes at the same time, unless you have the audio version of this book. Take a few seconds to breathe deep and get comfortable.

You're in a small room. Picture a card table with two boxes on top. If you want some ambiance, a fireplace is warm and crackling in the corner. A candle burns and smells *woodsy* with a hint of *spice*. Focus on the two boxes. They are noticeably different. The first one is called the *Value Box*. The other one is called the *Ego Box*.

The *Value Box* is plain and simple, about the size of a shoe box. No shipping labels, no fancy logo and no colored packing tape. Every person has this same box, this box will never change. Your neighbor, your friend or your enemy, the box is always the same. *All lives* have a *Value Box*.

Exhale, and take another deep breath, close those eyes and picture this in your mind. Embed it somewhere so as to see it often. This box is difficult to see or touch, but it can be felt and known. I will refer to this box many times. Wait. If you can't see it, how do you know it exists? Great question. Here's my answer: you can see the effects of this box. When you talk with anyone and strike a chord with their real value, they take notice. People will never forget your message about their real value, spoken or unspoken! Sometimes it will show up in their smile. Other times you may never know how it affected someone. I promise your message will not go unnoticed.

The second box is much different from the *Value Box*. The *Ego Box* has lots of labels. This box is different for every person, no two *Ego Boxes* have ever been alike. The sizes will vary and change. Unlike the *Value Box*, our *Ego Box* will never be the same for long. When you are five or fifteen or fifty years old, this box will look completely different, maybe not even recognizable.

The *Ego Box* can be damaged or destroyed and marred. It can be crushed, burned or run over. For sure it's fragile. We should be careful with this box. Let's not forget it's sacred and a marvelous creation, worthy of great respect.

The *Ego Box* is all about our external self. It's everything about you that can be physically touched or seen. It's our abilities and skill sets or lack thereof, it's our appearance, it's our culture and choices. Your reputation is in this box. If you're a thief or just plain lazy, it shows up in the *Ego Box*. If you're ambitious or successful, it's in this box. All the things you can learn and know are in this box. You can learn computer skills, plumbing, science, medical stuff, history, biology and a hundred other things. The worth and value of this box can change often according to the perception of ourselves or others. Kind of like the Stock Market, up and down but always volatile.

Always keep these boxes separate, or there will be problems. The clearer we see these two boxes separated, the less the *Ego Box* will affect our *Value Box*. Okay, got that image in your mind? Go ahead, I'll wait. Yes, it's important.

This may seem quite elementary, you may be thinking "Dude, let's just get some crayons and color us a picture"! You can use your own visualization if you would like. I'm just illustrating this so you can have an *image anchor*, as you become aware of how you perceive worth and value.

What about my leg?

To further explain about the *Ego Box*, suppose I'm a runner and break my leg! My internal dialog might look like this: "Oh, no, I broke my leg! I can't contribute to the team! I can't do what I used to do! I can't compete! I'm worthless, boo hoo!"

Hold your horses Elmer, let's examine the details more closely. Your *Value Box* hasn't been altered or even blinked. Sure, the *Ego Box* has a broken leg and yes it's going to be an inconvenience for a while. No, you can't contribute to the team right now. However, your value remains intact. This *Ego Box* tragedy can happen in so many scenarios, just fill in the blank.

I am or have been:

1. Hurt
2. Abused
3. Bankrupted
4. Divorced
5. Aging
6. Facing life changes

What a relief to know my *Value Box* is totally unchanged and not a scratch on it!

The *Value Box* is what I envision when I ask people how they view their own value and that of other people. Often, we confuse the commodity of our knowledge and skill sets (Ego Box) with our actual value (Value Box). These two boxes are ever so different. Be clear on this.

Responses have been favorable when I've had the opportunity to explain to people the theme and message of this book. Many people identify with the questionable message culture and society have been sending about their value. I'm amazed how quick a stranger goes into deep thinking mode and recognizes the idea of the *two-box* illustration for clarifying value.

The spark!

A young woman we know had a little girl several months ago. Natalia, what a sweetie. This event is what inspired me to think of the *Value Box* illustration. It was like a little spark kindling a larger fire. A day never goes by but what I don't think about this *Value Box* subject.

The mother was so excited for her family and the incredible event of birth. Seeing a child born into this world is beyond words. Anyone who has witnessed this says "Rolland, shut up you just said it's beyond words"!

So, I kept thinking about this ethereal event and a child's precious value. No question about the value and worth of little Natalia. Parents and grandparents know this drill. I thought about what my own children were teaching me about value. Would anyone question a child's worth?

Some gears began turning. When does this clarity of value change? When would her value be different? When she is a toddler? Or a struggling teen? Perhaps as a young woman having her own children? Oh, yeah maybe when she is a grandmother. Would this be the time her value, self-worth and soul value could drop a little bit. Absolutely not! This little child's *Value Box* never changes.

Not long ago a friend of ours died. She was almost 105 years old. She was an interesting person and had lots of stories to tell; Not all of which had happy endings. She lost two of her three children to sickness. Both were elderly when they passed away. A loss more hurtful than we would know, but she took this with courage and grace. No matter her age, she had the heart of a mother. Her children were just as valuable the day they died as the day they were born.

On a lighter note, our friend was so old she could remember when *Rat Fink* was the worst, meanest *fighting words* you could ever say to someone. When you heard those words, blood was sure to follow. Please excuse my foul mouth this once. Lucky for us such strong vulgar language isn't so common anymore! I can't think of the last time I heard those dreadful words!

If our value doesn't change, why have I not been aware of

this? Why does it seem like I just became privy to this information? What disinformation have I accepted? What messages have I been listening to about value and self-worth? Do I want to keep searching down this *rabbit hole* or just stay on the surface?

The answers to these questions rattled my cage for a while. Worth and value. Culture and society. Our own minds. Truth. Lies. All of these things seemed so tangled together. Questions remain, yet what *untangled* for me was the separateness of the *Value Box* and the *Ego Box* as aforementioned. This *thinking frenzy* became the inspiration for this book title: *The Value Message.*

It has been difficult for me to present this book with a flow or continuous story line. The content came about in a random fashion and has stayed this way. My hope is you won't find this too annoying. I further hope you would see the intention of the content. Which is to inspire colossal *awareness* of your value and self-worth.

That *four letter* Word.

A message in the Bible has always grabbed my attention. The word, "Word". One day I found out this four-letter word, "w-o-r-d" was more than what I had supposed. What is the "word"? The *Word* of God. "In the beginning was the *Word*". I just couldn't understand how this was often defined. Furthermore, I just felt dumb because how could something so simple feel out of reach. Of course, I couldn't share this with anyone, or I didn't share this with anyone. *Better to be thought a fool, than to open your mouth and remove all doubt.* This saying applied here.

I searched this out a bit. I'm not a good Bible student so I rely on the focus and brain power of those who are. The original Greek translates the word *Word*, to be LOGOS. Translated back to something I can understand is "message". Ah ha, this made so much more sense. A lot of depth is behind the meaning of LOGOS if you care to study this.

I'm not above reading the scripture in a way I want to hear it. However, inserting *message,* wherever *word* appears is just more accurate and helpful considering my placement on the

Smart Scale! Besides somehow being more aware of the *message* theme gave me another dopamine shot!

So now I see it from a different viewpoint. The Scriptures are referred to as the *book,* the *scrolls* or the tangible writing we can read and touch. No doubt, the scriptures are a message. It's possible however, that *the Scripture* and *the Word* are sometimes two different animals, with different meanings!

You wouldn't believe all the effort poured into the Scriptures throughout the ages. Most of the people who have been consumed with or appointed to this initiative have been detail oriented personality types. Now thankfully the world has some accurate and thorough information at its fingertips.

I'm putting this on the table for scrutiny, but here goes. The word *Word* appears in the Bible well over 600 times, if I researched this correctly. Most, if not all of those instances could or should be read as *message* (LOGOS).

1. God's *Word/message* came to…
2. God's *Word/message* was made flesh…
3. God's *Word/message* dwelt among us…

You get the *message.* This makes it more personal and pointed for me. I used to read the Bible and know what everyone else was supposed to do. Now I'm more apt to read the Bible and search for what I'm supposed to do. More apt to search for a message to me.

I add this about *the word* defined as *message,* to awaken your mind to being more aware of messages coming directly to you and your address. You are bombarded with messages every single day. Your unconscious mind is aware of this. Your conscious mind might not be so keen. Our unconscious mind, however, is not so discerning. Like your stomach, it just takes in what's shoved down the throat and starts to break it down. I guess you could say your stomach is quite *brainless.* Your big mouth is supposed to decipher what's good and bad, but as you know, the mouth still could use a lot of discretion. Likewise, your conscious mind is supposed to discern what is being shoved down the throat of its unconscious counterpart. Yet often discretion is lacking here also.

Train your brain to be a *gatekeeper* or filter. Learn to interpret the steady volley of messages coming to you. Think of the *true/false* tests you took in school. These simple tests didn't take much thought and only two options were available! It's true, most messages you are getting on a daily basis are either true or false.

For example:

You are...
1. A loser
2. Amazing
3. A joker
4. Ugly
5. Beautiful
6. An athlete
7. Clumsy

These words could be spoken by someone, by society or by our own selves. Such messages pertain to the *Ego Box,* sometimes the *Value Box*. Here is the perfect job for discernment, deciding which box these daily messages belong to. Some could pertain to both boxes.

For instance, you could say to someone, "You are amazing" or "You are beautiful my friend"! This message could apply to both boxes. However, "You are clumsy" is never going to apply to the *Value Box.*

The Fox Story.

For some years a unique message often perplexed me. I told no one about this except my spouse. What's with the fox? Yes, when someone I knew passed away, I would see a fox somewhere somehow. I'm not sure when I started noticing this but sure enough maybe one would cross the road or run across the yard. One time I saw one sleeping on the roof of a shed right at the place where we turned to go into the cemetery on the funeral procession route. How many times have you seen a fox sleeping on a roof? Not so often, right? Seeing the peacefully napping fox made me say, "Whoa, maybe not just a coincidence"!

Another time we were visiting some people and a red fox was running through the deep snow in their backyard, a beautiful sight on a clear blue day. I asked the couple who lived there if foxes came around often. "Oh yes", the man said, "they sometimes come up to the driveway and try to get in the garage". The same day I learned their daughter and son in-law lost their lives in a tragic accident some years ago. A few years later I wrote them a letter and explained my view of the fox connection. I never heard from them. Likely they just figured I was *off my rocker*. They might be right!

The fox theory was perplexing and intriguing to me. I wanted to ask someone about this but who would know? I took a chance telling the *fox thing* to a tattoo artist who was giving out Henna tattoos at a company outing in Florida. Figured she might know something about signs and symbols, and if she thought I was crazy, she was two thousand miles from my home and wouldn't know any of my friends or relatives! Sure enough, the tattoo lady had something fascinating to say! She listened to my story and said, "It's a message for you, just you, no one else. Other people would indeed think you were *off your rocker*, because the message isn't for them". This answer was a relief to me, and I no longer felt like I needed to explain this to anyone or be validated about something so unusual.

Chapter 2. Messages are coming!

Have you checked your messages lately?

Messages have always drawn my attention. Earth and humanity emanate communication in so many forms. Earth with its storms and volcanoes, its peaceful sunsets and calming meadows. Humanity with its groanings and turmoil.

No matter what we do, communication is unavoidable. Even silence is a message and often a loud one. We even send a message when we're sleeping. The message is: "I'm sleeping". It's just not reaching a lot of people.

You send and receive hundreds of messages every day, not including your cell phone. Your smile. Your frown. What you wear. What you eat. What you drink. What you say and how you say it. What you do. Let's face it, you're communicating every minute of the day. I'm sure there's a science for *message sending*. Would it be called *Messageology?* Whatever it is, I'm all about it even if it's sort of a *nerdy* study.

Observe messages we and others send. Notice if they are directed at the *Value Box* or *Ego Box*. With practice this will become second nature, because you're just a cool person!

Let's not forget the science of *message receiving.* This too is noteworthy. The clearest, loudest message is of no significance if it falls on *deaf ears*. Can you relate? Does anyone else find *messaging* an exhilarating study? Are you bored yet?

The *message within the message*! We are familiar with this sort of idea. Someone tells you something and by their tone or body language you know there's a louder message to be heard.

17

Advertisers are good at this. Whatever they are selling is going to make you look better, feel better, happier and more attractive to the opposite sex. These clever ads convey their messages with images, humor, catchy sayings and big promises! Mothers are professional grade too. Mom asks, "Don't you think you should wear a coat"? Don't miss the message within the message, which is. *Get a coat on, sooner than later, sweet pea.*

Getting the wrong message.

What disturbs me so much is the toxic message within the message when people suffer physical, mental and verbal abuse. The stinging, clinging message is: *You have no value. You are dirty. You are bad. You are not enough. You are worthless. You are an object, and a worthless one.* We know this list is long. The tragic Value Message here is: *There's no Value Message worth mentioning here.* These messages can be subtle, but their effects are devastating. At a young age this can be dangerously confusing.

Society and Culture do not have a good track record for letting your *little light shine.* Tread carefully, past and present history will tear at your heart strings. From enslavement to sex trafficking trades which have been both legal and illegal for centuries to genocides and atrocities littering the human timeline. A deeper dive into the dark corridors of *inhumanity* will put your emotions on edge, perhaps even leave the body weak and shaking for a while. If you are looking for a message about your value, don't look here.

"Sticks and stones may break my bones, but words will never hurt me".

This little rhyme is a test. Do you remember when you realized words can hurt more than broken bones? Congratulations. You passed the test. You now know, even though they are not tangible, words can be lethal. Move to the head of the class!

The message and outward hurt that comes with sticks, stones and broken bones, is straight forward. We may not be clear on the motive, but there's no question about the cruelty and anger. Nothing hidden and no subtle games to figure out.

Caustic verbal messages can be confusing and hidden. Disguised in many clever ways, their subtle cruelty covered up by humor or, "I didn't really mean it". These disclaimers and games can be brutal and hurt deeply. Don't underestimate the power of the tongue. With little effort this mighty muscle can unleash a withering swath of destruction.

Abuse perpetrates a crushing weight of loneliness, shame and humiliation, it's just too heavy to bear. Don't bear this heavy weight alone! Find the courage to reach out for help. Asking for help is not easy. I associate asking for help with humiliation at the least. Yet reaching out and asking, could initiate the change you've been looking for. This action step, or *asking step*, could help you realize *you are not alone!*

Loneliness. Shame. Humiliation. Depression, bewilderment and pain. Ouch what an ugly list, which will take a toll on your mental and physical health. Does this describe you or someone you know? Is abuse your comfort zone? Is this the predominant message you've been listening to? Have you rationalized your abuse? Telling yourself, "Maybe it's your fault" or "It could be worse". Are you convinced there's no hope for change? If this is you, I have some good news. Whatever your situation is, it can be different. Whatever your situation is, you have value. Keep one foot in front of the other. Walk toward the warm light of health and healing!

If you are in doubt about your value, it's impossible to ignore such a dreaded feeling. This inkling varies from subtle to dominating and can smolder for a long time. You can try to numb or hide your fear, but it will not go away. You will always be on the defense; behind the wall you've built. Terrified someone will discover your filth, thus blanketing you with stifling shame. This dread is here to stay and will come out another day to play I say, unless you begin to see your own value and the truth about your worth.

It's so important for you to see and understand your value and worth, forward motion depends on it. Your health and sanity are at stake. You may not know this yet, but forward motion *doesn't* depend on *others* seeing your value. If other people see your value, it's simply a bonus.

Chapter 3. Why you are not amazing.

How can you become settled and clear about your own value and worth? What do you believe about your own value? What messages are you believing and listening to about this value? It's not the messages you hear, but the ones you believe that create your reality.

The reason you are not amazing is the onslaught of messages coming from abuse, society, culture and your own brain. These message bearers are not your friends. Such messengers condition you to see and judge with the eye using the standard of the *Ego Box*. Rarely even acknowledging the *Value Box*.

Our conversations and thoughts are tainted with finding ways to make ourselves (our *Ego Boxes)* look good and other people (their *Ego Boxes*) look bad. Jealousy and envy live on this street. Maybe it would be accurate to say your *Ego Box* is quite amazing, but you are much more than just your *Ego Box*. Your *Ego Box* could be full of talent and capabilities. There's no question about the phenomenal gifts that come from the *Ego Box*. We spend hours of *screen time* watching *America's Got Talent* and the like, just to prove this point. However, it's still only an *Ego Box*.

You all have examples that come to mind when thinking of an *Ego Box* gift. The *Human Camera* is such an example. Stephen Wiltshire. Stephen is on the Autistic Spectrum, yet he has a gift which earned him this title of the *Human Camera*. He can remember what he has seen with astounding accuracy. The

21

documentary I watched took place in Rome, Italy. He was flown around Rome in a helicopter for Forty-five minutes. All he did was look out the window the whole time. Afterwards, he spent three days in a large room with a panoramic drawing board, maybe thirty feet in length. On this board Stephen drew details of what he recalled from the helicopter ride. Absolutely stunning would be a terrible understatement. The accuracy of roof tiles, windows, streets and buildings is mind blowing.

What is your gift? Do you know what this is? What do you do well in service to others? Your gift doesn't need to be something that makes the newspapers. Discover what your unique offering is. For Marie Calendar it was making pies. Colonel Sanders liked to fry chicken. Imitating someone else's gift won't be genuine or graceful. Trust me, you have something to give. Realizing your gift will give you a *special place* to focus some energy.

Yes, the gifts and abilities of the *Ego Box* are just about endless. Yet if this is only what people see and know us for, we won't feel too stellar. Culture idolizes people for what they can do, not for the depth of who they truly are. Masses of humanity are hungry to be seen and heard. When this doesn't happen, these masses feel let down, not even close to amazing. The Value Message here sounds sort of skinny, no meat on its bones.

Messages on the *negative bandwidth* are like a steady ticking of a clock. Annoying at first, but sadly, after a while we don't even notice. If this is where you are, any positive vibe will seem unusual. We could be so comfortable with negative messages that we repel anything positive. We'll never believe what we don't understand. *Belief* is the key here. Whether the messages we receive are negative or positive, the ones we *believe* are the ones which influence us.

Pause and consider which messages are easier for you to believe about yourself. Negative or positive? This is a great step in the *self-awareness* direction. If you get just a hint of a negative message, isn't it all too easy to believe? Even though it may sting, you're just so sure it's true. Furthermore, you throw some more dirt on top of it. Digging up your known character flaws and other godawful baggage.

Yet when a positive message or compliment comes your

way, what then? You like it, but it's just too good to be true you are certain. If the message is recorded or in print, you'll play it over again and again, but you feel like there's no way it could be true. It's like test driving a new car that's out of your price range. You fantasize while driving the Range Rover around the block a few times. In the end you resign yourself to returning the key because there's no way it can be yours.

I'm not saying we shouldn't be open to criticism or feedback. We aren't always right and who doesn't need to improve something about their character or personality? If you can be clear about your value, it will be easier to *filter feedback.* You will have a better idea of which to apply and which to discard.

Keep your *Value Box* separate from both positive and negative vibes. Regardless of what you tend to believe about negative or positive messages, neither has to affect your worth and value. For instance, you can be clear about your value, whether messages directed toward you are positive or negative. This will take the edge off extreme highs and lows of daily living.

Culture and society have a vested interest in connecting your value with your *Ego Box.* If you can be persuaded that your value and worth are connected to your abilities and skill set, you will buy the product and chase the approval of others. Like a hound on a rabbit. A lot of running but not a lot of meat.

If you buy the product, in reality your *Ego box* may be improved but your *Value Box* will not change. For example, you might get a closer shave, yes, the new perfume will smell fantastic, or those shoes will improve your running comfort. Your value is not altered by any such purchases.

When I was looking for my first car, mom and dad told me what the actual purpose of a car was. It's for getting you from point *A* to point *B*, no need for the *bells and whistles,* they'll cost extra. What do you mean, Dad? I had no idea the purpose for a car was so simple. This was definitely a surprise. Why hadn't my friends and the car salesmen told me this? All this time I thought a car was a vehicle for inflating your value to new levels. BC (before car) I felt like a loser and a nobody. A drifter with no meaning and no chance of girls noticing me. My expectations for a car were much more than just point *A* and *B.* I knew a car would improve my life and let me tell you I was very knowledgeable for my age! I would be willing to spend beyond my means for a vehicle, it would be so worth it. A car would send my value through the roof. I'd have clout, friends would be envious. Neighbors would have newfound respect and be more tolerable of loud music. A cool looking car would make me feel like a grown up, yet with not too many responsibilities.

I guess mom and dad knew something about the trappings of the *Ego Box*. After the *shine* wore off, and a few parts fell off, I could reluctantly see their *A* and *B* points. No matter the car, you are still the same person but now have car payments.

The Perfect Storm!

Another high achiever on the *why you are not amazing list*, is: perfectionism. Oh, this hurts just thinking about it! This never achievable goal is responsible for much inward anger and frustration. Perfection is not a *maybe* or *rarely* achievable goal, it's most definitely a *never* achievable goal. Be clear on this too.

Drop perfection like a smokin' hot potato! Lots of research and development exists on this topic (Perfection, not hot potatoes), but seriously, make getting over this a priority! Who knows where it starts but be clear on where it stops! I hereby give you permission to be free from perfectionism and whoever it is you are trying to impress. Feel the release deep in your belly, breath deep and get some rest! The facade of perfectionism will not serve you well. Your perfection is not likely to help anyone, especially you. For the record, I say this with a nice tone of voice and from a place of empathy.

Our nine-year-old got a shirt for her birthday, the caption read: Practice Makes Progress! I love it, this specifically is a message created to dismantle the age old saying, *practice makes perfect.* How often have we chased the dream of practicing long enough and hard enough to be perfect at something? *Practice Makes Progress* lifts a heavy load. With practice my efforts can now reach something attainable.

People pleasers may have the biggest challenge with this animal. Always anxious to do what someone else wants us to do, naturally sets us up to be manipulated and unhappy. People pleasing has been around for generations as a means of survival.

Unlearning the responsibility to make others happy will mean a mindset adjustment. Be kind to yourself on this journey.

People pleasing is defined as: *our sole purpose is to make others happy*.

Look at the gold stars you get in school. Every student's name on a chart, if you are good at pleasing people, you get a star. You are a star! Or so you think. We can't wait to look good and look at who is not so good. Some boy always shows up who could care less about stars and even tries his best to keep them off his neat little row. He's the carefree happy one most of the time. So, at a young age we hear a message about our value. Stars mean I have value, in our *minds' eye.* Lack of stars means I don't have value.

Star value can only be applied to the Ego Box! Implying that more stars equal more value should be examined. Can you see the *carrot on the stick* here? Problems and confusion come along when our *Value Box* and *Ego Box* are not separated. We connect our self-worth with the gold stars.

Over achievers get caught up in *this storm* also. Whatever you have done or accomplished, *it's not enough.* Whoever you are, *it's not enough.* If you have heard this message from society and culture, it's time to throw some awareness into the ring. Be aware of the messages you have been listening to. Ambition is admirable if it's for the right reason, listen to your inner dialogue. If the driving force for you is because you aren't good enough, or it's not perfect, and it's never perfect or good enough, you need a break. A break from this mindset.

If you don't become aware of your *Value Box*, you will picture your worth like the stock market. *Up and down! The market* being the highs and lows of whatever other people will bid for your value. This *market driven* mentality is stressful and exhausting. When your own stocks are low you can be overwhelmed and depressed. If panic sets in, you'll sell out. You will be vulnerable and apt to do some crazy things to inflate your stock price and gain short term approval.

Does this sound all too familiar? Would you consider an alternative? How about getting out of the market altogether?

Investments exist with much better returns, I promise. Invest in yourself, find people who can help you acknowledge your worth and value. Lead by example and show people how to treat you.

Perfectionism, people pleasing, and over-achieving doesn't have a Value Message, but needs one. One sounding like this: *Your value is still intact, and we love you, even if you don't do it perfectly. We even love you with your imperfections.*

Six Sisters Stuff.

A few years ago, we bought an *Instant-Pot.* A kitchen appliance, sort of like a Crockpot on steroids. You can cook a whole chicken in twenty-five minutes and look like a genius when your company arrives.

Searching YouTube for recipe ideas, I came across the *Six Sisters Stuff* channel. As you might guess, the contributors are six sisters. Maybe you found this family already. These ladies share recipes and household tips for viewers. They have tons of videos on easy Instant-Pot recipes that add spice to your life. Their channel is hugely successful. Most of the videos have millions of views. Why is this channel so outstanding? These girls have got their stuff together, but that's not it. The food is good but that's not it. They are all good looking, but that's not it either.

The reason the *Six Sisters Stuff* channel has hundreds of thousands of subscribers is, they are not perfect. Yes, they live in fancy homes, they know what they are doing, they smile a lot, but clearly, they are not trying to be perfect and most importantly they don't want you to be either. Their gift is putting viewers at complete ease. It's in the mannerism and wording. They say stuff like, "I do it like this, but you can do it however you want, and it will be totally fine. I use chicken broth, but beef broth or water works too, *you just do you*". It's impossible to write on paper the intonations and manner in which people speak. Look this channel up if you can and see if you agree. Fans don't feel like they are competing or at all need to have a perfect finished product. You will leave their channel feeling comfortable, empowered and in no way judged even if the chicken burns a little bit. The *Value Message* here is: *It's not about the chicken, it's about you and the relationships you develop.*

Mistakes. Rare, medium rare or well done?

"A mistake that makes you humble is better than an accomplishment that makes you arrogant." -Anonymous

Mistakes are costly, they cost time, cost money and can cost our dignity. Fear of mistakes can cause paralysis and stomach upset. Mistakes are associated with humiliation and failure. These are hallmarks of *missing the mark* or a dreaded misstep. Mistakes, however, are champion teachers!

Doing the wrong thing is how we learn best and how we learn often. Society and culture reinforce the punishing aspect of making mistakes. This fear of being shamed can be torturous and crippling. I've heard the message about learning from mistakes for a long time. Heard motivational quotes and read inspiring stories about how individuals learned the greatest lessons from a fall.

These days I'm more apt to listen to messages regarding the wisdom of mistakes, listening calms my fears. In our mind, mistakes can leave us stranded and left for dead. Truly the schooling we get from doing the wrong thing is of great worth, let that sink in.

The message mistakes leave you with may sound like this: "Are you nuts? You aren't even close to amazing." Get a grip, grunt or whatever you need to do to shut the door on this message. Those mistakes will repeat themselves until we learn the lesson. The lesson being a gift to be thankful for. All your mistakes will not alter or mar your *Value Box*. However, they will give your *Ego Box* some *black eyes* unless you look for their blessing. Pick yourself up, brush off the dust and *buckle up Buttercup.* You have a brand-new sunshiny day ahead and so much to learn!

Dysfunction. Fortunately, it's always someone else's fault.

Who isn't exasperated by dysfunction when we see it? Trouble is, when it's in us we don't see it. It's always the other person or other family *slapped* with this label. What are some hallmarks of dysfunction? Enabling, power tripping, passivity, passive aggression, bullying, tantrums and a whole host of other not so nice things. Wow, my blood pressure is rising. These menacing behaviors are costing lives and aren't going away anytime soon!

One definition of dysfunction is: half of the entertainment industry. You know by now; I just need a lot of dopamine in movies I watch. Why is so much dysfunction puked into our brains from this source? Dysfunction has a lot of gray areas. Let's not fall into the trap of wanting to be the perfect family or person because this perfect model doesn't exist. The *perfect* family doesn't help us learn or grow through difficulties and real-world scenarios. A *Leave it to Beaver* utopia would have its own aches and pains.

What can I learn here? I can learn that dysfunction is a product of the *Ego Box.* I can learn to not judge. I can learn to be aware of my own dysfunction, which I have been blind to. I can learn to choose courage instead of cowardice. I can learn to not be surprised by the cause and effect of such dysfunction. I can learn to think for myself instead of having the media or other people think for me. Well, shucks, there's so much to learn here I feel like going back to school. A great lesson for me is when it comes to humanity, we learn three things.

1. What to be like.
2. What not to be like.
3. Leave it at that.

Consider the entertainment industry, do you ever watch movies and get so involved you just want to throw a chair through the window? I used to get so agitated either about what was going wrong or upset about my time being completely wasted. Or I get so excited for what's about to happen, I just can't sit down. It's not much fun to watch movies with someone like this. So, I thought I'd try to be more relaxed and ponder what might have happened differently in the movie. Instead of being so intense, just breathe deeply and be more *okay* with whatever happens in the plot. I'm not a control freak of course. Stories just always go better if they turn out exactly like I think they should!

Ghosting in the closet.

Ghosting is a socially dysfunctional problem and topic right now. Which is more noticeable because of social media. Ghosting is when you are best friends or in a relationship one day and you disappear the next. You don't answer calls or respond to texts. Whoever you are ghosting is frantic, wondering what they have done wrong. Or thinking something terrible has happened to you. Simon Sinek at simonsinek.com brings some attention to this practice. Simply turning your phone off for the evening to unplug is not ghosting, by the way.

Believe me when I say I'm familiar with avoiding difficult conversations. Bamboo shoots under the fingernails sounds more appealing. What does this behavior say about how we see the other person's value? It says a lot, says way too much. I only recently heard the term *Ghosting.* I write about this because the effects can be hurtful and leave you second guessing your value and worth.

If you have *ghosting* inclinations as I do, think about the message this sends. Not to mention the lack of courage exhibited here. Difficult conversations are difficult. Therefore, they are called difficult, right? Facing your fears is the only way to get through them.

If you are being *ghosted*, consider the source. Communication isn't easy, the message here is telling you something about the other person. When someone reveals who they are, believe them the first time. Your worth and value doesn't need to be shaken.

Clique it or ticket!

Cliques are a *thing of the past,* but also a thing of the present and an easy trap or habit to fall into. Everyone gyrates toward people they know or share common interests with. It's safe and it's dopamine. Are cliques intentional and mean? This grouping behavior is so the opposite of *inclusion and diversity.* Yet I'm never sure if cliques are intentional or accidental, but they are all too common. Cliques or clans have been around for thousands of years. It's the safety thing and has been a means of survival for centuries. No judgment here, just love, but how can we bring awareness and solutions to the table? How can we avoid this abusive *team player* game? How can we be more curious and less judgmental about other groups?

"The greatest thing that will come out of your comfort zone, is *you*." *-Anonymous*

Usually, we get good vibes when we network and get the courage to reach out to the *other side*. You know, connect with the shy people, or sit in a group of people you don't know. Just to see what happens. Most of the time everyone is glad for the exchange, appreciative when someone demonstrates courage. Let this be a lesson for me and help me see opportunities to dissipate the clique mindset.

You might guess something about the *Value Box* would show up here! Let's start in school, where the *clique skill set* easily develops, there's no shortage of this societal behavior. Such skills will continue to follow us until retirement. Unless we become conscious of this and actively learn new behaviors.

I will refer to Dr. William Glasser here again. His work produced some remarkable results in the education field. Dr. Glasser authored at least three books specifically about education.

Glasser, William Dr. *Choice Theory in the Classroom.* USA: HarperCollins, 1988

Glasser, William Dr. *The Quality School: Managing students without coercion.* New York; Toronto: Harper & Row, 1990

Glasser, William Dr. *Schools without Failure.* New York: Harper & Row, 1968

He advocated giving students the tools to foster better relationships which is a great remedy for *clique mentality*.

Warning: Dad joke, coming up: Tempting someone to join your clique, would this be *clique bait*?

Glasser advocated relationships first, academics second. Guess what happens to academics when relationships take first place? Academics improve immensely. Are you surprised? Of course not, who doesn't do better when the environment is extremely conducive to learning? Do you know how much more Rocket Science can be learned if students aren't discouraged by dysfunctional relationships? I recommend any of Dr. Glasser's writings. Do yourself a favor and indulge in some research on this inspiring author at wglasser.com!

Don't we cling to our own group because we want to shore up our personal value and self-worth? In the comfort zone of our *clan* is safety, validation and camaraderie. If we break into another circle, we run the risk of harassment, embarrassment or looking like a total idiot. Or we risk being shunned by our circle of friends, ouch! If someone breaks into our group, it's the same thing in reverse. They fear the worst. They risk harassment, embarrassment or looking like a total idiot. Either way the threat of vulnerability is high and will feel too much like having a tooth pulled. Our first response to looking outside of our circle is usually not so pleasant!

What if you knew everyone in the other clique worried about the same thing? Or better yet, you knew they all had a *Value Box,* and you could help them become aware of it. Furthermore, what if you understood how to not focus on the *Ego Box* when referencing the other person? When you are settled about your value, threats are less worrisome. When you see and speak to others value, they in turn feel less threatened. You might be surprised to find, *the walls* built by anxiety come tumbling down.

Beauty And the *Ego Box* beast.

Speaking of cliques and power trips, you could think pretty girls are the meanest. Sometimes true, plenty of movies and stories paint this picture. If you are that girl, the attention might be fun, but what a heavy weight is on your shoulders.

Naturally our eyes are drawn to beauty. Whether it's people or nature or architecture, many things have the *draw* of beauty. Fame, beauty and money are strong *people magnets*. If you possess any one of these, you will draw *followers* and *likes*. Will these *followers* see your *Value Box*? Unlikely. Will this get old and feel lonely? Likely. When people are enchanted with our *Ego Box*, relationships will be shallow at best. Getting a lot of attention isn't the same thing as connection! No reason to be jealous of someone else. The person you envy may look like they are having a ball, but it might just be a *ball and chain.* Just because the other person is amazing doesn't mean you are any less amazing! The supply of *amazing* isn't limited nor will it run out any time soon.

So, if you know someone who is famous or beautiful or has lots of money, be kind to them. Without seeing their own *Value Box,* they might be in crippling fear of losing this slippery *Ego Box Euphoria.* Sometimes their unpredictable behavior is a way of trying to cope with life.

"We're starving for connection, *not attention!" Bridgett Devoue*

What a great quote, it helps explain why people do what they do. I find these words so true when reflecting on my own life and actions. I want to look at this from another angle. How about this?

"We are *starved* for connection, but sometimes *settle* for attention."

Attention comes in many forms, some of which can be abusive. Haven't you wondered why some abuse victims come back for more? Or others just endure this abuse for way too long, never finding the courage to walk away. Never understanding they are far too valuable to tolerate such misuse. Maybe a clue can be found here. I wonder how many abused people would say, "I was starving for connection, but I just ended up settling for attention even if it was abuse".

This quote also makes sense of why boys tend to show off, for connection not attention. I'm just thinking out loud. Boys have an extra gene which compels them to show off whenever girls are around. It's hard to say if seeking connection or attention is at play here, maybe both. Guys are not opposed to extra

32

attention. *Connection* just has a better ring to it, when trying to explain some of the Idiot things boys do when a girl shows up!

Chapter 4. Hate no body!

The Apostle Paul said, "No one yet hated their own body". Oh, yeah? Have you ever hated your own body? Maybe. I have talked with people who were a mess of emotions and histories who seemed to deplore their body. Seeking to be released from it, they cut it, or sought to destroy it in some way or another. My question is: did they hate the body? Or did they not understand their value? You can be imprisoned in such anguish and emotional pain, that any next step or other option seems impossible. Bitterness and anger toward our own self can be a comfort zone. As a result, we can't even imagine any other way to be. Our negative self-image becomes a defense mechanism. For instance, we could demean ourselves as a preemptive strike. Striking before someone else gets the chance. "Ah, ha, I got me before you got me!"

Was Paul referring to the physical body? After all, we feed and wash the body, and nurse the body when sick. So, what's up with hating the body? Maybe it's what's in the body we can be so hateful toward. People who cut themselves are clearly harming the body, yet they don't hate the arm or wrist. It's something within they lash out at or hate or at least are frustrated with.

Maybe you have serious regrets about some choices in the past. Everyday a gray cloud covers your sky, keeping the sun from view. Is something gnawing at you? Something you feel can't be shared. A weight, literally crushing you, slowly but surely. This will lead to self-loathing and anger, directed inwardly. Don't go down with the ship! You may or may not be hurting yourself physically, but without a doubt, you are destroying yourself psychologically. I implore you, take steps toward freedom that comes from seeing your worth and value.

Our youngest, the seven-year-old, had a secret to share. It was heavy on her heart. She had taken a shower and somehow cut her finger. We thought it was a razor, but she denied this when questioned. Claimed the sharp edge on the drain was the culprit. A few days later she fessed up to the truth, indeed it had been a razor cut. She was so relieved to feel heard by her mother. Afterwards she said to her mom, "It feels so good to tell the truth". I think we can all relate to this message and the peace that comes after we open our hearts. Bless the children and please find someone you can confide in if you have something weighing heavy on your heart and soul. Don't wait for tomorrow.

If your body and mind have been subjected to abuse, the steady message you have received sounds something like this: "*You are a loser, lazy, dirty, revolting and worthless.*" This message is far too easy to believe. There might even be lots of evidence to support such labels. Just because you get knocked to the mat doesn't mean you need to stay on the mat! These negative messages have become your comfort zone, in a twisted way it feels good and feels true. I promise, you weren't born to stay on the mat or even be in the ring. You can come up swinging but if you stay angry and frustrated, this will only keep you in the ring. Everywhere you show up will be a boxing ring.

Anger and frustration may serve you well at some point. Anger, for example, can be the catalyst which propels you forward, perhaps helping you *draw a line in the sand.* Anger and frustration will not change other people. You can waste staggering amounts of energy trying to change someone else.

Hate and anger are both formidable opponents. Don't be intimidated, they are powerful yet have a great weakness. All the anger and hate in the whole world can only destroy. It can never help or heal. Love on the other hand, is bristling with both power and might, one of the strongest substances known to man or woman. Only a half-ounce of love can dissolve *mountains* of hate and dissipate *truckloads* of anger. Only love has the capacity to heal and give hope. Love is alive and giving, it brings life to everything it touches. The spirit of love will never die or be extinguished. Hate brings death to everything it touches, it has only one destination which is the grave.

Stand up and be counted.

Learn to advocate for yourself. Why? Because you are worth it. Standing up for myself (or others) has not been my strong suit. I've been quite cowardly over the years and I'm still ashamed of it. I have to be vigilant about this to not be a repeat offender. My first recollection of this is being bullied in grade school. I didn't have the courage to stand up for my brother or myself. Oh, I could have lots of excuses, but I'll just own it and say I sucked at advocating, and it showed. The message about my value I was listening to and believing: *Not much worth am I, not even worth enough to stand up for myself.*

One of my good childhood memories from this difficult stage of life was when a big kid named *Frankie* moved to town. He and my brother became good friends. Frankie's favorite sport was terrorizing two of the kids who bullied my brother a lot. He could do this with one hand tied behind his back and blindfolded! His day was always happy and bright when he could chase and catch those boys somewhere. I guess I'll always remember Frankie's attitude as one of advocating for others!

My definition of advocating for oneself has changed over time. Labels I used to associate with such audacity would be someone not fitting in or simply making waves. Someone who is selfish or arrogant. Someone putting their needs ahead of others or not a team player. For sure we can't know the truth about motives, but I no longer am offended or intimidated when anyone speaks their mind. More power to communication. More power to advocating for yourself.

Our youngest daughter is a great teacher of advocating. Sometimes she would climb into bed between her mom and I and we'd playfully refer to her as the *pickle in the middle.* One morning this happened, she was still sleepy. One of us said to her, "You're the pickle in the middle". She jumped up in a flash and screamed angrily, "I'm not a pickle in the middle", dropped down and went back to sleep. Whoa, sorry there, grumpy bear. Didn't know you were having a bad day already. Good job standing up for yourself!

Even when she is awake, her ability to describe her feelings is remarkable. "You made me sad", or "You hurt my feelings". Straight to the point, no apologies and no matter who has offended. This communication style will serve her well. If you are the boss or the husband or the neighbor, it doesn't matter. You will be held accountable for what you do and speak.

Yes, I own that. Owning vs. Renting.

A friend who worked as the deputy assessor in Shoals Indiana was telling about an older couple coming into the office declaring every detail of their property. While most would be reluctant to declare all this detail in fear of paying more taxes, they were not. My friend sensed a pride of ownership as they dictated all the measurements of their house and outbuildings. Of course, they wanted to pay the fair amount but also it just felt good to own property.

Many people rent property. So, which is better, renting or owning? Both have their *pros and cons.* "Drive it like a rental"! You've heard or thought this before. Implying you have *no skin* in the game if you are renting a car. No worry about repairs, warranty or longevity. *It's not my problem,* could arguably be a legitimate mindset. You can walk away from rental property with little or no emotion invested and even less money.

So, let's think about our actions and behaviors. We can be owners or renters. With a renter mindset, we have some expenses to cover, but the experience is mostly worry free and responsibilities generally fall to someone else.

Ownership however is a different *ball game.* You are responsible for expenses, taxes and utilities. If you leave the lights on, guess what? Who pays? You do! Tax bill shows up in the mail, yep, it's all yours. You can't blame your neighbor for your taxes or utilities. If you did blame them, guess what else? The bill still shows up in your mailbox! Water heater leaks, toilet overflows or the roof needs replaced. *Who ya gonna call?* Ghostbusters? Wrong. It's all you baby!

However, what also goes with this is the opportunity for pride of ownership. You can make your house a safe, comfortable place for neighbors, children and friends, even in-laws if you care to. No one can stop you!

When it comes to behavior and actions, the sooner you choose to become an owner, the sooner you will start seeing real changes in your life. Ownership is empowering. Ownership moves us away from the victim mindset. Ownership points us to the virtues of self-care. Ownership can help us set boundaries. Ownership can lead to self-awareness. Ownership will help you understand the meaning of responsibility and improve relationships. Owners know how to communicate effectively, apologize, be truthful and accept accountability without blaming others!

Abusers: Great power but not great responsibility!

Abusers are notorious for wielding great power over their victims, often for years or even years after the abuser is dead. Victims can remain in a victim state months or years after an incident. Abuse is like a drug to an abuser. Whether its power like a bully, sexual abuse, verbal abuse or otherwise, abusing people is like a hit of crack cocaine. It feels so good to make ourselves look big and others look and feel small. Dopamine shows up again! Abusers are addicts, one of many labels which could be applied to their *Ego Box.*

What if I am an abuser, addicted to getting my high from someone else's pain?

1. You can admit you are an abuser.
2. You can decide to change.
3. Own the responsibility for your actions and don't accept your excuses.
4. Triggers are not someone else's responsibility.
5. Chose to treat people with respect, publicly and in private.
6. When people hold us accountable for our abusive behavior, it will seem like they are attacking us.

This is a start. The journey to self-awareness is long and steep, too scary for some people. Look for the *Value Box* in others. Understand that it's not your responsibility to control other people. In fact, there is great freedom when we can *let it go!* If you are serious and want to change and not just be sorry, contact your nearest local Domestic Abuse service. Other people can help you, but "Only you can prevent forest fires". -*Smokey the*

Bear. In other words, you alone must be the one to change.

After researching domestic abuse, I felt the need for some self-examination. This process became painful upon the exploration of my *blind spots.* I asked myself, "What abusive behaviors or traits do I use and why?". I was directed to Patrick Weaver at patrickweaver.org (Patrick Weaver Ministries). I follow his posts on Facebook. Patrick's posts are hard core, pointed and very searching. He grew up in an extremely toxic environment and has made it his mission to free people from such a painful place and hell. I've never read such a thorough, granular definition of *malignant, narcissistic abusive behavior.* I found myself asking deep personal questions. Why and when do I exert the need to control people? Do I feel like it's my responsibility to direct someone else's life? Do I treat my spouse and children the same in public and private? Would I treat others differently if I knew someone was watching? Suddenly I felt more responsible to be authentic and genuine always. Not just when other eyes were looking.

I was encouraged so much by this man because our thinking is similar. I too share a deep concern for abuse and violence entrenched in society, yet willingly ignored or swept under the rug. Especially abuse perpetrated behind closed doors. I had just forgotten a very fundamental detail. The prerequisite to examining others is to examine oneself!

Ironically, abuse victims feel responsible for the devastating effects of abuse. Typically keeping all the pain, confusion and hurt inside, victims have difficulty opening up about abuse. Such conversations get complicated quickly. For example, sometimes people fear loneliness more than abuse, so they are not motivated to change their situation. If you can be tuned into your real value and self-worth, you will be in a better place to put responsibility where it belongs.

Maybe you were drunk, or flirting, or jealous. Maybe you didn't display your best self, perhaps the moon wasn't lined up. What if you were irresponsible or negligent? Who cares? Responsibility of abuse belongs on the shoulders of the abuser. It's okay to stop making excuses or enabling, because the legitimate excuse for abuse does not exist! Okay, maybe the abuser is working through problems. Problems of their own, they did or did not create. This in no way absolves an abuser from complete responsibility for their actions. Abusers are controversial. Abusers have little interest in self-awareness, growth or improving relationships. *Abusers are renters, not owners.*

Safety is no accident!

This catchy slogan appears often in company safety departments. I want to add a word about your personal safety. Be clear on your intolerance for abuse, but don't be naive about your situation. Lisa Nichols shares so helpfully about a *life-threatening* relationship she was in; Life threatening to her son and her own self. Firstly, I'm glad she safely exited this relationship. Secondly, I'm thankful she had the courage to put this in writing for any who might need a similar game plan. This was a life and death matter, a time to use your mind not your mouth.

When *Reality TV* first came out, I watched tragedy unfold. So did thousands of other viewers. It was traumatizing to me. Now I can watch reality TV and not even blink, how sad.

A lone female police officer had pulled over a large male suspect and his maybe ten-year-old daughter. Both were asked to come to the back of their vehicle where the camera recorded all the *gory* details. Instantly I could see what was up and about to go down. In my head I was screaming at her to get a clue and get out of there. The male suspect was clearly agitated and getting more so by the second. She mistakenly thought she was the authority in this situation and acted like it. Raising her voice, giving orders and taking names. Oblivious to the pending danger. The officer was in this guy's face like a barking hyena. Twenty feet wouldn't have been far enough away from this volcano on the verge of eruption. The young girl with this guy was extremely anxious knowing full well what this man was capable of, she was literally jumping up and down with fear and dread.

The first blow happened like a bolt of lightning, knocking the officer totally unconscious, she literally didn't know what hit her. Blows continued to rain on the way to the ground and after she hit the ground. The suspect and girl got back in the van and left the scene, leaving the officer for dead. Clearly traumatic for this young girl to witness such violence, likely not for the first time either. To my disbelief the officer lived to tell her side of the story. A year and many surgeries later, she was still not able to return to work. Her injuries were severe.

Is it testosterone? I'm a guy, is this the reason I could see what was coming, *a mile away*? My first reaction to this female officer was beyond negative, seething with blame. Not being able even slightly to comprehend how she couldn't have the least bit of a clue. Even thinking about it now, I'm trying to evaluate the evidence for answers.

Was this a *rookie mistake*? Was she arrogant and a control freak and expected everyone would *toe the line*? Do some women have a *blind spot* regarding the capacity for male violence? I truly don't know. I'm exposing my *blind spot* in saying I cannot see how the outcome could be so overlooked. However, it was indeed overlooked and what can be learned?

This man was so responsible for his actions, he was at fault, he was violent, he was wrong, and he threw the punches. Yet the officer was irresponsible for her actions. What an excellent training video but too horrific for any curriculum. If such a needed sense of *situational awareness* is not there, can it be taught or learned at all?

If you are involved in a violent relationship, consider an intelligent exit strategy. Appreciate your value enough to vacate the premises. I'm not lying, an exit plan will take loads of courage and stamina. Not to mention wisdom and humility. Don't lose heart, you're worth it.

"Sometimes courage is holding on. Sometimes courage is letting go." *-Unknown*

If it's not broken, don't fix it.

This clever saying has always befuddled me. Oh sure, I get the message. If it's currently working, the wise path might just be to keep it working, even though issues are present! Change is difficult. The situation might be more complicated than you realize. Besides, fixing takes time and energy. Sometimes money!

Yet, *fixing,* is so satisfying! Bringing a junkyard car back to life, is a story of hope. What once wasn't wanted is now appreciated. Solving a problem that stumped someone else, feels invigorating. Salvaging a wreck after a stranger tossed it in the garbage is empowering to the *fixer.* I watched an intriguing YouTube video a few days ago, it seemed out of place at first. The YouTube Channel was *Rainman Ray's Repair.* Video Title: *Tale of a self-made man.* This channel and many like it, show tips, tricks and experiences of automotive repair techs. *Cult level* followings and unbelievable stats on views and subscribers show up here. Fixing things draws a crowd and learning something always justifies the time you spend *glued* to the screen!

The video was captivating, it was literally a nature walk in the woods, appearing to be mid-summertime. The cameraman (Ray) was telling about another mechanic friend of his and his not so pleasant childhood. A documentary style story of how this guy overcame dysfunctional experiences as a child. As children, both had traumatic experiences. Truly broken experiences to be exact.

As they were visiting about their lives, a profound statement was offered about why they like to fix things. "We fix things, to keep from breaking ourselves".

These guys, like many others, seemed drawn to the trade or gift of fixing what is broken. The more I watched the video, the more it didn't seem out of place at all for a fix and repair channel. The more it made sense, why millions and millions of viewers are loyal to this genre. The more I knew there would be a place in this book about *fixing what is broken.* The more I could see the eloquent *Value Message* coming from Rainman Ray's video recording. *Fixing what is broken* is a recurring theme in this book.

There's so much I didn't know about writing a book when starting this project. Publishing, editing and grammar can be intimidating, but getting to use a trendy word like *genre* is a plus. Deciding which genre would apply to my book was somewhat confusing to me. So, I broadened it and say, *Psychology, self-help and/or inspiration.* However, there may be a new genre category which would accurately describe the mission and purpose of this writing. The *Fixing What is Broken* genre!

People are hungry for solid evidence of their value. The blindest person could clearly see this solemn truth. Another arguable truth is that humanity and brokenness are synonymous. Culture, society and our own selves attempt to cover or deny this truth on a daily basis. Cover and deny is something humans learn to be extremely good at. We use a variety of drugs, activities, shopping, busyness, consumption, lifestyle and a truck load of other things to cover and deny what is difficult to touch. For many, deep down, brokenness is a throbbing pain, so naturally anything numbing the hurt is worth exploring.

Just ask my brother, *covering it up doesn't make it go away.* When he was a child, matches were a lot of fun, so he lit some pine needles on fire. He got bored and covered up his little fire with a bunch more pine needles and walked away. After a while, dad looked out the window and said, "Hey, I wonder what the fire trucks are doing here"? Of course, my brother said, "Yeah, I don't know either". Neither of us boys were a *George Washington,* believe me! Just sayin' covering up our pain points will not put out the fire nor solve the problem. Lucky for my brother, no one was hurt, and the fire was contained to some pine trees and a few bushes. He didn't tell the *truth and nothing but the truth* about this incident for a few more years!

Rainman Ray's deep authentic conversation came from an unexpected place, and I was struck by this. Should I have been surprised? No. There were some confirming messages for me, and you probably recognize them.

Firstly: People often think deeper and are more spiritual than we give them credit for. Deep thoughts are called *deep thoughts* for a reason, they don't quickly come to the surface.

Secondly: We cannot possibly know the hurts someone might be wrestling with or trying to cover up just to substantiate their value. Don't be quick to judge with your eye or mouth.

Thirdly: Some people have never heard a positive message about their value, or one at all. This is why being intentional and kind with our words is a *no-brainer*!

Fourthly: The nagging question about self-worth will consume and drive some people to prove their value and worth. A relentless, honorable and commendable drive. Yet a drive that will seem like a never-ending journey, one without a destination.

More conversation about this topic might *wear the horns off a Billy goat,* but I've been thinking about the term *broken.* Broken could imply that somehow the victim just wasn't able to hold up. Shame on you for being weak and faltering when flooded with overwhelming dysfunction and defectiveness. If an abuser has broken you, do you feel defeated? Still humiliated and ashamed that you weren't strong enough? Does it feel like you let yourself down and you can't seem to apologize enough to make it right? Would some stronger wording clear the air? How about this: *You are hurt and in need of care!* This wording puts responsibility for abuse a bit more squarely on the shoulders of the abuser.

If your leg was broken in a car accident, would you feel apologetic because your body couldn't stand up to the forces of nature? Of course not. Just like the results of abuse, see it for what it is. *I'm hurt and I need help, I need someone to care.*

Here is a Value Message for you: *Stop! You have always been valuable. You have never, not been valuable. I see you and your value. I don't need proof! Go get some sleep!*

"Kindness... don't leave home without it!"

Chapter 5. The Dopamine conspiracy.

The dopamine conspiracy!

Dopamine is a predictable behavior driver. You will understand a lot if you know about this marvelous chemical. With a little observation, you too will become aware of what I call *The Dopamine Conspiracy*.

You don't realize it, but Dopamine has infiltrated many areas of your life. Without your awareness or signature this chemical is controlling much of what you do. From our bank accounts to our plans and actions, we just hand over the reins and go along for the ride!

What is Dopamine doing in this book? Dopamine is a type of neurotransmitter, sometimes called a chemical messenger. Let's bring some serious awareness to this topic. Let's explore how addictions of any kind prevent us from helping people see their extraordinary value.

Let me mention here a book written by Dr. William Glasser.

Glasser, William Dr. *Positive Addiction.* USA: Harper Collins, 1985.

The writer explores real addictions that have genuine positive effects. Dr. Glasser looks at two particular case studies. Running and meditation. The author goes into great length about how addictive traits can have a positive connotation. He chose these two subjects because these activities are commonly known to be addictive. Typically, addiction generates a negative image. This book brings a positive light to a negative subject.

Addictions have a way of directing our priorities. Become aware of the messages you are sending. "My addictions have priority right now over you." This could be the message we are sending, which doesn't speak well to people's intrinsic value. Speaking a message to someone's value is like speaking a different language. It's easy to learn though, you can start by practicing on yourself! Go ahead, you have my permission to say some positive things about yourself. When you become more aware of your value, you gain a more empathic world view. You can better understand how your actions impact others and what messages these actions send.

Power is an addictive way to get a sizable dopamine shot. Making ourselves feel big and others small, always gives us a quick hit. Clearly smoking this Dopamine (Dope-of-mine) is harmful to others, yet I still find myself trying to make others look small in subtle ways. Take the time to become self-aware in this arena. Old habits die hard.

A common social mantra might be: *we get our pleasure from your pain*. This can't help anyone, only hurt them. Power struggles and meanness happen at the expense of the other person. We get a Dopamine high from such behavior. Although without this drama where would we get ideas for books and movies? The evening news would only air for about ten minutes, including the commercials! The Value Message coming from putting people down to lift ourselves up is naughty, not nice.

The truth is, we can be addicted to a lot of substances. Items most of us don't associate with addictions. Anger. Drama. Attention. Stress. Pain. Power. Sympathy. Shopping. What can you add to the list?

Is it the substance or is it the results? Think, Dopamine! Ok, if I'm hooked on something, alcohol for example, I love what it does for me. Sure, I don't like the hangover, but I like everything else. The numbing of my problems. The attention. The camaraderie. The excuses. I'm not addicted to the actual alcohol. I'm addicted to the effect and how it serves me.

Is it not the same with other addictions? My high doesn't come from the *substance* so much. It's not the power or drama or anger or being mean. No, it's the shot of Dopamine I can't get enough of. Crack is the high of choice for some, but oh so destructive. Yet for others peer approval, stress, anger or something else is the high of choice. Perhaps not so devastating, but an addiction, nonetheless. Again, no judgment here, just observation.

How about your favorite movie or video game? Not too many movies have an unhappy ending. You can endure the good guy getting beat up because you know in the end your *Dopamine* fix is coming. He's gonna come up swinging, he'll be just fine!

About fifteen years ago, I read *The Hunchback of Notre Dame* by Victor Hugo. Thinking how sophisticated I was for getting into the classics.

Hugo, Victor. *The Hunchback of Notre Dame.* New York: G. Munro, 1879.

Spoiler alert! Dopamine is not at the end of this book, not much in the beginning either. Just when you fall in love with Esmeralda, too! I have never forgotten when and where I read this book. I didn't want to get out of bed for a week! No, I am not kidding. This is how difficult it is to face life without my Dopamine at the end of the story. *The Hunchback of Notre Dame* should be banned or at least carry some warning label. *Warning: Dopamine Deprivation Ahead!* Incidentally, Quasimodo, the *Hunchback,* (one of the main characters) was rescued from infanticide. Tragically not an uncommon practice in those days. I was more *historically naive* back then, but all I'm asking for is a little more Dopamine in my reading material.

Society is not well versed on how to deal with difficulties and situations which offer little or no Dopamine. What is your method of coping when the *going gets tough*? What happens when the picture in your mind is different from the reality in front of you? Where do you learn the skill set of coping? Where is the class in school teaching this? Problem Solving 101. Wouldn't the world change if this class showed up on the curriculum next year? Sure, in the movies it all works out, but that's just following the script. Our favorite actors always show up with creativity, solutions and a plan. How do you learn to think like this? How do you exercise your brain so problem solving skills are cultivated? Being afraid of success and an avoider hasn't served me well in this area. I had to try something entirely different!

Ernest Shackleton and dopamine.

At the recommendation of a friend, I read a well-known survival story about an expedition to the South Pole in 1914. The captain and crew became trapped in the ice, seeking to explore and cross the pole.

Lansing, Alfred. *Endurance: Shackleton's Incredible Voyage.* USA: Basic Books, 2014.

This book made an impact! I proposed to reduce my many instances of complaining and *belly aching*. Furthermore, my meager happenings of gratitude needed to rise quite sharply. Any crown of perseverance I have ever mustered up, I lay down at the feet of the captain and mighty crew of that ship.

NEWS FLASH! Seriously! today 3/10/22 my brother sent me a text about Shackleton's ship: Endurance. I'm not lying. He just heard on the news about Ernest Shackleton's ship being found at the bottom of the Weddell Sea, near the Antarctic Peninsula, in relatively good condition. I was ecstatic. Big, big news for me, this is one of my all-time favorite stories.

I also just discovered shackleton.com. This site has a plethora of Shackleton history and information about the crew members. The website also sells a line of clothing for your expedition. *Shackleton* is the name of the clothing line, how original! Durable and rugged, but the clothes don't make the man or woman, don't forget this when your boat sinks!

Here are some highlights from this trip lasting over one and half years. The ship, which did have a lot of food stores, became stuck in the ice. Also, they brought along a new kind of vitamin briquette which kept their teeth from falling out and aided their health.

1. Twenty-nine men on board.
2. Spent over one year stuck in the ice before the ship was

crushed and broken up.

3. Sailed three lifeboats over 600 miles to a desolate uninhabited island. Elephant Island. Seven-day trip! I can just hear the guys in the back saying, "Are we there yet". Still to this day the island is not a tourist destination! Population: 0

4. All but six men lived under the two lifeboats on said island for over four months while the other guys sailed on rough seas 800 miles to get help at South Georgia Island where there was a whaling village.

5. After landing on the wrong side of South Georgia Island, Shackleton and two others hiked over treacherous terrain 32 miles to the whaling village.

6. Fun fact, the men became consumed with thinking about food. Every night they would talk about one recipe. Talk about if they had eaten it, the different ways to do so and all the details; just like Bubba did in the Forrest Gump movie! Talked about all the ways you could eat shrimp. Do you remember the scene? The beginnings of The *Bubba Gump Shrimp Company.* Penguins doubtfully, was ever the food topic.

7. The only navigation system was a sextant. Which basically tells you where you are on the planet based on the stars and the day of the year. Sailors use a similar device these days, called a *cell phone!*

8. After the good food ran out, the only source of meat was penguins. Good thing they weren't at the North Pole (no penguins there). Penguin fat was fuel for the stove.

9. When the ice got warm enough to be *slushy,* they could take a bath.

Also, I found two spiritual lines from this book to be quite remarkable. The first statement was this. The men credited their salvation to their Captain. Fondly telling of his care for them, his leadership and empathy for each one. The captain helped everyone care for each other. Kept them occupied with duties and entertainment, never losing hope despite such dire circumstances.

The second noteworthy statement was a compliment.

After so many months at sea and over four months on Elephant Island their captain showed up with help. A rescue ship, able men, food, blankets and maybe some soap! Shackleton said he received the greatest compliment ever bestowed to him. His men said, "Captain, we knew you'd come for us"!

These men placed their trust and faith in their captain. They loved him and knew the feeling was mutual; not because he said so, but because he did so! Put yourself in the shoes or boots of those men on Elephant Island, waking up every morning subjected to seriously harsh elements, barely surviving frostbite. Can we grasp the mindset here? Not thinking, every single day truly *sucks*. Instead thinking *This could be the day, this could be the day the Captain of our Salvation sets his foot down on this forsaken island!*

Let me learn the lesson of endurance! When little Dopamine is to be found, we must change our mindset. Can you also put your feet into those boots and feel what must have been felt when the rescue ship came into view? A Dopamine shot of all Dopamine shots. The Value Message spoken and heard from their captain during and after this ordeal looked something like this: *You are of incredible worth. You are worth any pain. You are worth any hardship. You are worth any sacrifice and any price. Your value is without question. I would give my life for you!*

Learn the skill set of coping and problem solving when the environment is harsh. Learn the *happiness* which comes from long-term perseverance and struggle. Not the short-term *shot* of Dopamine.

For more information, do a *web search* on *Dopamine Detox.* This is an exercise in awareness and stamina. Just observing how Dopamine affects people is educational. Detoxing from Dopamine stimulants for a whole day will take a lot of *umph*. Honestly, I tried this for half a day once. What a terrible experiment, but it opened my eyes to the effect of Dopamine on my behaviors and decisions.

Chapter 6. The world's best teachers.

Children are the world's best teachers.

Children easily teach us important lessons about our value. When having conversations about value with people, I find three themes always emerge... always!

1. It's easy to see the worth and value of others
2. It's difficult to see our own value.
3. Children help us think about the meaning of worth and value! Maybe it's a niece or nephew, but they have a message for you.

Isn't this amazing? Children help people think about worth and value. Do children preach this message? Do children write a story explaining the details? Of course not. You got the message loud and clear, possibly a few seconds after your child was born. Haven't you just marveled at children? Watching them while they sleep? Appreciating that they aren't talking back! Wondering why they can't be so sweet and innocent when they are awake. Thanking God for the schooling we get in the midnight hour of silence. Lessons so valuable, soul reaching and soul teaching that words couldn't begin to explain. Yes, my friends, people can teach us a lot of *tricks and trades* in this world, but children will teach us about real *soul value*. We can't choose our parents nor our children, but we can choose to see their value and worth.

As a toddler he or she will bring joy and frustration. As a teen, maybe she will bring this also. What if she wrecks the car, turns to drugs or is a gifted sports player? How about when your son accidentally throws a rock through the neighbor's window? What if your daughter can do nothing with a ball at all even though she's tall? What if she goes to college and drops out or is the valedictorian? As a young juggling mother running a business, looked up to in the community, what if she just totally rocks it? What if she blows it? What if she is expecting a child in high school? How about friends? Maybe she will have many, maybe few. What if she is a cheerleader? What if she's not? What if she struggles with her own sexuality? What if your son steals from the candy store? What if he is in an accident and is horribly scarred? Or tragically your daughter was abused sexually or mentally, or her grades just suck. What if she doesn't get many *likes* on social media? Everything here pertains alone to the *Ego Box,* which changes often and is quite unpredictable. A lot of *what ifs* here, but we can always learn from children. We can always learn more about the *Value Box* and how to send a value message every chance we get!

None of the preceding paragraph has anything to do with the *Value Box.* Nothing has changed about this box. Look for opportunities to gift your child with a message about their intrinsic value. The message may look like a hug, a smile, a phone call or text. You can be creative because hope and kindness is a language anyone can speak. Speak it often and speak it fluently!

One of the great things about children is they aren't aware of the *Ego Box.* Before I was school age I remember sitting on my grandma's lap and putting my hand on her chin whiskers, carefully rubbing my hand on them. Isn't it terrible to talk about my grandma's whiskers? Or is it? Years later she recalled me doing this and was curious about the reason. I found it comforting somehow and likely was simply exploring textures as a child would. Just saying, children don't give a rip about *Ego Boxes.*

As grandparents, a lot has happened to your *Ego Box.* Age isn't too kind. Hair grows where it didn't before. Or doesn't grow where it did. Pain shows up in unexpected places. No wonder grandma doesn't even ask if it's ok before showing you pictures of her *little cuties.* She's so proud of them, they see her *Value Box* with perfect clarity, not seeming to even notice the diminishing of the *Ego Box.*

Lemonade Lessons.

A few years ago, our girls set up a lemonade stand when we had a garage sale. They were so excited to try their entrepreneurial skills. Saturday came and so did lots of people. It was picture perfect, cold lemonade, hand lettered signage, cups and smiling faces.

This was my first run at lemonade sales and my education level was about to go up a notch. Immediately I learned two things.

1. It's not about the lemonade.
2. It's about how you treat my kids.

I thought of myself as amiable, wanting to get along with anyone. Until I watched how people treated the girls at the lemonade stand. Some people were all too happy to engage with these waitresses, some simply ignored them. Mostly guys in their forties or older, the grandfatherly instinct kicked in I'd say. They thought this was all too cute and wanted to encourage capitalism. Some didn't even take the lemonade but gave them a few bucks anyway. Mostly women, looking for a bargain were the few who didn't even notice the refreshments or simply ignored the girls altogether.

I was sort of shocked at my weakness of character, the amiableness I had assumed was so ingrained, was nowhere to be found. To those who weren't nice to the kids, my defenses got stirred up.

To those who treated the girls favorably, I felt differently. They could step on my *blue suede shoes*, no problem. Once strangers, now lifetime friends. I concluded that we all, our children included, could learn something from people, whether they could see our *Value Box* or not. This balance builds character.

Little Brother Lesson.

Let me share another lesson a child taught. Some years ago, my wife and I signed up for a match with the Big Brother Big

Sister program. We were assigned to a little kid with a big, big smile. We all went to a restaurant to eat one evening. There was a group of people eating and visiting. I tried to sit elsewhere because our *little brother* never met a stranger, but I wasn't always sure what he was going to say to people. Sure enough, the first thing he does is ask why they are all here. It was quiet for a few seconds, and someone said, their child had died a few years ago and they were all gathering for a birthday celebration to remember this child. I then suddenly noticed this dozen or so people were quite sober even though birthday party plates and balloons graced the table.

Those words hit my gut, I didn't know what to say, I didn't know what our little friend would say, emotions might be difficult for him. So, he says in a clear and genuine voice, "I'm sorry". Those people were quite touched by such heartfelt words. Rarely have I witnessed seeing someone so *in the right place at the right time.* This is what it means to *live to impact, not impress.* I had no idea so few words could mean so much. It was obvious those folks felt the same way. The Value Message here: *Empathy is always in season and needn't be complex.*

Pets are the world's second-best teachers!

Did you hear about the man who left his house and fortune to his beloved cat? Everyone shakes their head in disbelief. Yep, left a few million in a trust fund to be doled out to the kitty cat. You know the bumper sticker on his fancy car read: "The more I know about people, the more I like my cat!"

This makes total sense. Pets do not see your *Ego Box.* Cats are still a mystery to me, so I'll be switching to *Rover* soon. Cats don't see either box, but they are soft and furry and keep the mice away. Occasionally they let you into their world and space which is enough for owners to get a fleeting sense of love and belonging. If those owners haven't had good experiences with humans and are rich, the cat just might be throwing a party. Wouldn't it be great if you got an invite to the *Heir Ball!*

I won't spend much time on how deeply a dog understands the *Value Box* concept, but no question about their ignorance of your *Ego Box*! Our daughter had cynophobia (fear of dogs), this was worrisome and seemed unusual. We were encouraged to learn her pediatrician shared this same phobia until she was twenty-two years old. At which point she adopted and rescued two dogs of her own. What a great action step to face fear. Our two dogs rescued us! Cynophobia is no longer a worry in our home, but sometimes I end up in the *doghouse*!

Dogs are master communicators even though they only know one word which is: "Bark". This is dog speak, which means: "You know the *Ego Box* humans are 'head over heels' about"? "Yawn"! Oh, this is the other word dogs know, "Yawn", and that's what dogs think about the *Ego Box*. Pet lovers are a peculiar people and support a billion-dollar industry as many businesses know. Pets are dearly beloved for their entertainment and companionship. Mostly because these *companions* are unaware of any faults and care even less about your *Ego Box*. However, if you need a realistic balance, I have a suggestion: Own a dog to worship the ground you walk on and a cat to completely ignore you. The Value Message here: *Figure it out people. Ego Box, litter box, same thing to your cat!*

.

Chapter 7. Let there be no doubt!

This line from the dedication of this book feels so refreshing and powerful. I hope it does for you too. When you finish this writing, I hope you will stand up and scream this from the rooftops. I hope you feel the truth of your value in your bones and chromosomes!

One of my favorite Bible stories has always given me astoundingly good vibes. You don't even have to be a Bible fan to appreciate the point. (1 Kings 18:22 KJV). You can look this up instead of my paraphrased version. For many years God's people fell prey to idols and false god worship.

The story goes like this, there was a false prophet named Baal who influenced many to false worship, immorality, etc. So God's prophet says… "Let's all meet at a certain place and decide who the real God is". What a great idea, seems fair, I mean who knows for sure these days.

Everyone agreed about this plan and wrote it on their calendar. Yep, the God who answers by fire will be proven beyond any shadow of a doubt to be the real McCoy!

So, the time and place was Mount Carmel. Fun fact, it hadn't rained for three and a half years. Elijah didn't have a monstrous fan club, tensions were at an all-time high, nevertheless everybody wanted to show up to check it out.

Baal's prophets started first, went on all day, cut themselves, danced, screamed and generally *whooped it up.* When nothing happened, Elijah mocked them. He said, "Maybe your god is sleeping or traveling and missed the bus or something".

After Baal's prophets had their fair shake, Elijah spoke up. There was an altar on scene, and he had someone pour a bunch of water on the whole thing so as nobody would accuse him of foul play or some secret pyro trick. Elijah uttered just kind of a quiet prayer (1 Kings 18:36 KJV). No dancing or cutting, no hoopla and no circus. What happened next could never be forgotten by anyone who witnessed the *message* coming down from above!

There was no confusion, no "Well, yeah but maybe". There could have been no words of protest or wondering of any sort, not in the least. Just put yourself in a front row seat to this event and take in all the sensations and feelings of such a display. Close your eyes but don't miss the show!

Fire came down from heaven, consumed the sacrifice, the wood, the stones, the soil and licked up the water in the trench as a finishing touch. The stones… read that again! When have you ever seen a fire hot enough to burn up stones and dirt? Just what I thought… never in all your born days! Now who could ever make you doubt or *unsee* such an event? Pity the fool who would try and convince you of anything other than the truth your own two eyes witnessed here!

Can you digest the vivid and unquestionable reality and truth of such an experience? How unwavering and lacking in doubt would you be every time the story was retold? How unmoved would all the attendees be when faced with mockery and questioning of others who weren't there? You could tell the story without emotion or drama. None of this would be needed because you wouldn't care if people believed you or not. You would know for sure what happened because there simply IS NO DOUBT!

It is with this same intensity of NO DOUBT that I hope you are able to understand and see your value as absolute and without question. Realizing your own value is the *Game changer* of *Game changers!*

Why you *are* so amazing.

Just look at you, truly a gift, you are amazing. Look at the people around you. The gift of the body for instance. Human anatomy just blows my mind. 206 bones, twenty five percent of which are in the foot. All the organs, muscles and tendons work together every day. Think about the gift of dexterity and grace. Your body is built to run, jump, crawl, walk and fall. Your hands and eyes automatically coordinate to catch or throw a ball or simply write a letter. Body parts, a brain, involuntary functions. Fingers, able to move and grip. Hands with the ability to help and heal. For some of you, hair grows out of your head, no effort on your part.

All this information is stored in a seed so small it's scarcely visible under a microscope! When the conditions are right the seed grows into a most complex being. Armies of scientists can only find more things to study and discover about this life form. The power of science still never coming close to understanding everything about this marvelous gift and creature.

The capacity of your mind is *mind blowing!* Your brain will never be able to compete with the speed of a computer. Don't fret though. The computer will never be built or conceived with the ability to do what your mind is capable of. A computer is only a box of pieces and parts. No more no less. You, on the other hand, can think freely. You can develop relationships, show emotion and demonstrate empathy. You can understand people, their hurt, their humor. Your body can heal, your hands can heal other bodies. Your smile and hug can heal. Your ears can read between the lines. Feed your confidence in this area. Be grateful. Gratitude is something else a computer can never grasp. You are truly a gift. Life is a gift. Be clear on this. Don't let technology *push your buttons* or intimidate you!

Oh, and another thing, creativity. Look at the arts and all the clever inventions in the world. Profoundly spectacular. Do you remember the old TV series: Gilligan's island? A group of friends shipwrecked on a desert island. The professor was always creating something to improve their lives. If he could build a radio out of two banana leaves and a coconut, why couldn't he just fix the boat?

Recognize your creative gift. Find out what this is and explore it. Creativity is therapeutic and can be relatively inexpensive. Don't believe me? Just ask someone what their hobby is. Watch how they light up and can't wait to tell or bore you with their interest!

Arrogance vs. Amazing.

"There's a thin line between confidence and arrogance…
It's called humility, confidence smiles, arrogance smirks." -
Unknown

The difference between arrogance and amazing. Let's take a close look at this *odd couple.* One might question the wisdom of lavishing anyone with compliments or praise. If you are like me and have been stingy in this department, you have a whole list of reasons to hold back. Your motives could appear as manipulative or patronizing. The reason I think of most is, too much *nicey nice* could make people arrogant. Good point. Is it? As if we should be overly worried about psychologically scarring people with over complimenting.

Well, here is my answer. It's too late! Arrogance has already arrived. If you are arrogant, it's not because of *nicey nice*. It's because you are simply conceited. Complimenting people rarely if ever fosters arrogance. In my experience, genuine approbation produces humility and gratitude. People are arrogant long before someone has said something nice to them. Arrogance does not serve us well. This trait will not help you connect on a deeper level and will lead down a lonely pathway.

Chapter 8. It's time to tell the story.

A message from your local Fire Department!

I'm grateful for some lessons learned while serving on our local volunteer Fire Department. What Fire Fighter hasn't watched hundreds of hours of YouTube videos where you can learn even more lessons about priorities and value?

People over property.

This is the general sentiment among firemen (People over property). It didn't start out this way for me. At first, I was so taken up with the *apparatus*. Meaning the big red truck, the air pack with the cool face mask. Learning how to operate under pressure. Preparedness and how to survive in harsh environments is super important, right? So, *people over property,* what's up with these words?

Any Fireman worth their salt, has watched three or four hours of *Fire stuff* videos on the internet. We know this number is much higher, ok massively higher, but let's not tell our spouse.

In one such video, there was an apartment fire with two children badly hurt. The officer in charge put them in the only fire truck on scene and headed to the hospital. Leaving the building to burn and to be taken care of by the next arrival. There was some opposition, but the officer said, "*People over property*" and off he drove. The Value Message here was quite clear: *You are far more valuable than where you live!*

All that matters.

Another time the tones went off just before I was leaving for work. As I drove to the Firehouse, I could see a serious column of smoke rising hundreds of feet into the air. Never a good sign. A house trailer was on fire, *fully involved.* Meaning survival isn't possible.

Let's listen in on the radio traffic and empathize with the 911 dispatch operator. Their only picture is the one you paint with your mic. I couldn't be a dispatcher. My emotions get *out of hand* too quickly for such a line of work. Responders and dispatchers know painfully well, not all stories have a happy ending.

Engine #8: kkctch (radio noise), "Mt. Sterling from Engine 8."

Dispatch: kkctch "Go ahead, Engine 8."

Engine #8: kkctch "Mt. Sterling, Engine 8 is on scene."

Dispatch: kkctch "10-4 Engine 8."

Engine #8: kkctch "Mt. Sterling, we have a trailer fire, fully involved… all occupants are out of the structure at this time."

Dispatch: kkctch "10-4 Engine 8."

Ok, now imagine if you will the dispatcher sitting in a large box, probably no windows, recording all the details, tension is high. It could be dangerous and who knows what chaos will unfold. Kkctch "All occupants are out of the structure at this time" has a happy *ring* to it! So much so that I'm going to replay the radio traffic as it might be heard from the other end.

Engine #8: kkctch (radio noise), "Blah blah blah blah blah."

Dispatch: kkctch "Go ahead, Engine 8."

Engine #8: kkctch "Blah blah blah blah blah blah."

Dispatch: kkctch "10-4 Engine 8."

Engine #8: kkctch "Blah blah blah blah blah blah blah... **All occupants are out of the structure at this time**."

Dispatch: kkctch "10-4 Engine 8."

Just sayin', if everyone is out, the other stuff is "blah, blah, blah". Be safe, spray some water where you can and call it a day!

When we pulled up to the fire, my eyes caught a glimpse of the occupants outside the structure. A father and his little girl, maybe seven or eight years old. They were just calmly leaning against the fence watching the scene unfold. Wow what a loss, they didn't have much to start with and now it was all burning to the ground. The look on their faces was my value lesson for the day. They had each other, which was a lot. Certainly, all that mattered. They were speaking a Value Message to each other without uttering a word. The Value Message here: *I love you. Everything is going to be okay.*

Right then I decided I didn't care about your property. I can't speak for other Firefighters, but I'm guessing my thoughts won't be too far off. When it comes to property, I'm not enchanted with what can burn to the ground.

At least once a year, our fire department set up a *safety house* at the local school. A small house on a trailer which could be filled with fake smoke and students. An educational tool to teach fire safety.

We'd ask kids what the most important thing is in their house. "Is it dad's gun cabinet or home theater system? Is it mom's China cabinet or the living room furniture? Is it your toys or your pet? No, *you* are the most important thing in your house!" This is always the correct answer! No exceptions to this Value Message: *You are more valuable than your house and everything in it combined. Don't forget this, it could save your life!*

The farmer in the Dell.

Ok, let me tell one more fire story and I promise to go on to the next subject! One hot summer day we got two calls for field

65

fires at the same time, at different locations. The one we responded to was started by a hot bearing on a round baler. About five acres and six or more bales were on fire. Fire likes hot and dry anything. Anyway, we worked on this for about an hour before it was under control and *stomped* out.

While we were getting equipment cleaned off and put away the farmer came over to talk. He was worried and apologetic. He had beat himself up pretty good about the whole thing and asked how much this would cost, clearly thinking the worst-case scenario.

We've all been here at some time or another. You know, you did something you wish you wouldn't have, it's embarrassing. Who beats you up the most about such foibles? You guessed it, your spouse. No, seriously, you are the one who does this. You immediately jump on your *negative loop, I'm such a dork* wagon and nearly kill the horse on the way to town.

Kirk Fuqua, one of the Firefighters seemed to know the man and assured him that paying taxes was enough and being in the Fire Protection District, there would be no charge. Reassured him he had done the right thing and thanked him profusely for even calling us. Kirk, speaking for every fireman on the planet, said "We're just here to help". My takeaway was another valuable message. Our farmer friend got the message too. *You are what's valuable, not your property*! Be clear on that and don't kill the horse!

One man's junk is another man's treasure!

This brings excitement to life and city-wide yard sales. Your neighbors and grandparents are all too familiar with this truth. Maybe they are some of *those people* who slowly cruise by your garage sale before the doors are open. You can feel the hope in the air of everyone dreaming about finding some great treasure in exchange for a few measly dollar bills. Oh, the beaming pride you hear in the stories about how Uncle John bought the two bottle jacks he had been looking for. Only $4, what a bargain and no extra cost for the dirt and grime covering such a nugget!

Now doesn't this sound all too familiar. Our tendency to

under-value our fellow man is so smooth and natural, we see it every day. Not unusual and again no judgment here, just an observation. We may highly value our friends and family but assign no or little value to people across the planet or riding their bikes down our street. Just remember the child or person on the other side of the earth is someone's greatest treasure.

As a hypothetical experiment let's go find a *biker dude*, you know maybe a grandpa, *Harley rider*, the one with arms twice as big as your legs. He just rode into town to see his grandkids and brought his granddaughter a brand-new bicycle. He'll drive miles just for a hug, which is more value to him than a mountain of cash. Ok, so while his little grandchild is riding her pedal bike through your newly seeded grass, you angrily march out to tell her not to ride there. You look frustrated. Just before you get to her, you trip over a tree root. Falling onto the bicycle. You try to catch yourself, but the girl and bicycle spill on to the ground. Tragically for you, Grandpa now thinks you purposely knocked his little *snuggle bunny* from her bike.

While the *biker dude* is making a pulled pork sandwich out of you and crushing large bones, do some thinking! You can think about how much better it would be to treat another person's treasure with a bit more calculated kindness and care. Yet don't be so alarmed when someone doesn't understand what you treasure.

My Father's work.

A few years ago, at work a World Food Day was announced. Anyone could bring a dish from another country or culture. Some of my family heritage is Syrian so I brought stuffed grape leaves, yum one of my favorites! We had a simple brown pottery dish I used, everything fit, and it looked so *Betty Crocker*.

Just as I was walking into the meeting room with said dish, a lady excitedly asked about the dish. The container, not the food inside. "Is it Canon Pottery? It must be, I'm sure of it. I'd recognize it anywhere." She was over the top excited about this. I knew her quite well but was taken aback by her energy. You see her father was a Potter, well known in the area and she had grown up with this artisan influence. Of all the dishes at the table, she recognized her father's work instantly. She noticed it above all the other containers and pots at the table. Didn't even give a second glance to any of the other dishes. Clearly this made her day to be reminded of her dad's work and touch at the wheel, perhaps childhood memories.

What if we could instantly recognize our father's work? Pick it out among all others. All other dishes and containers are like the attributes of the *Ego Box.* One dish (vessel) alone is the work of God. Do we recognize this container in every individual? Do we see this dish as the *Value Box*?

Here comes more help.

God sends help but never, ever in the way you think it will happen! Whether it's wisdom or growth, maybe an answer to your question. When has God sent you help in a way you were expecting? Never, that's when. You can thoroughly comb through the *Black Book,* but you will not find many, if any average events.

The *average expected* way would feed your ego. Something would happen, or a message would come to you, and you'd be like, "Dude! That's exactly what I expected. I guess I know so much. God sure jumps when I speak." You'd go on your *merry way* and never learn a single thing. Never having a clue about how *small picture* we are and how truly *big picture* God is. We would miss so many incredible opportunities to learn about things outside of our world and comfort zone. Speaking of comfort zone, never miss an opportunity to get out of there!

Somewhere around 2006 I was wanting to connect more with people and the deeper world around me. How is this done? Where do you start? The internet, churches, perhaps Walmart or a Coffee House? Be careful, of course, wherever you search, because people can be scary! I'm aware of scary people as the news portrays this so well.

However, some *scary* people have made a favorable impact on my life for which I'm thankful. If there was a device that could test for *scary* people, we'd be surprised at who they are, or who they aren't! There was a post on Facebook just today that read, "It's so hard to find people who will work, it's now ok for *Long Haired freaky people to apply!"* You have to be old to get the song reference.

Walmart, Evansville Indiana, early 2000's. I once was plagued with panic attacks. While at said Walmart one afternoon, I started to freak. It wasn't the crowd, as there were about twenty people in the whole store. It wasn't the government, there were no Federal agents in sight. Hmmm, must have just been me and my own mind set. Anyway, for sure I couldn't get to the door fast enough. About fifty feet before I could get to the car, something else made me panic. A stocky, large black man was walking directly toward me with gusto! Could have been a brother to Shaq, maybe he was, for all I know! Dressed in a clean button-down white shirt, mirrored sunglasses and black pants. I know you have to watch out for those *scary people*, but other than running there was no way of avoiding his trajectory.

I wasn't prepared for what happened next. When he was close enough to reach me, he stuck out his big hand for... a handshake. Yep, looked me right dead in the eye, shook my hand and said, "Sir, I hope you have a great day!" That was it, he walked away and into the store never to be seen by me again. Probably went on to scare a few more people. I hope so. There it is again. Help comes in ways we do not expect. The best part of this story is, I've never had another panic attack. Guess he just scared them right out of me. Or were my eyes starting to open to the power of connection? Either way let this be a lesson to me! You don't know whose life is going to change because you told them to have a great day! The few seconds it takes you to be kind could last a lifetime for someone! Kindness is contagious, don't worry about the results, just look for the opportunities!

"I wear it for the one whose bad trip left them cold." *Johnny Cash* "The Man in Black".

Perhaps these lyrics from *The Man in Black*, apply to a man on death row I corresponded with. Such a heartbreak on many levels.

A series of documentary style newspaper articles caught my attention. This was in Evansville, Indiana (Courier Press). One man's tragic choices cost a family their lives and landed him on death row. The article gave an account of what happened and some general information of this inmate's situation. The news reporter shared details from her personal interviews with this guy. At the time he'd been on death row for twenty-three years.

Now before you get your *undies in a bunch,* hear me out.

I thought to myself, *what if I just look at this situation without judgment.* Maybe only curiosity this time. Let's see what happens. Guess what happened? I found myself more empathetic and less hateful.

What happened was tragic, no question about it. Think of a sister who looked up to her brother. An older brother who was the friend and confidant a teenage girl would need. Then one day the world stopped turning for her. A nightmare she can't wake up from begins. This awful dream happened because your big brother made some terrible choices.

Everyone knows. Your neighbors know. Your teachers and classmates know. Everyone knows it was your brother on the morning news. You can't avoid the stares or not hear the whispers behind your back. It's painfully clear that few if any people in your world see your value, much less your self-worth.

I tried to put myself in this girl's shoes. It hurt. It was confusing. It was lonely. I hoped someone took her aside, offered her a warm hug and said, "I am so sorry for this mess". I'm guessing icy stares were more commonplace. Our actions are not always our own. What we do affects our surrounding peeps and could be devastating to those who look up to us.

In no way am I attempting to take away or lighten the hurt and tragedy of those who lost their lives. My mind has trouble getting wrapped around such an event. I have total sympathy for the family and friends touched by such recklessness. The effect of tragedy is far reaching.

I struggled about even sharing this sad but true story with you. No Dopamine, no happy ending in sight. Where is the Value Message? How about this man's sister? Because of his frightful actions she now has no value in the eyes of the community. I struggled with putting this story anywhere in this book. I received two letters from this man before his life was terminated. The only line I remember was this; "Thank you for remembering me in my folly."

Not judging here, one shouldn't be surprised. After all, the community is also trying to sort out something that will never make sense. Many would act out of fear. The *Fear Factor* has long distorted the human psyche. Fear causes us to act out in ways that don't make sense. Fear can blind us to truth and reason. Fear is too deep a subject to tackle here. Fear can be our friend or enemy, but either way it will always be along for the ride. Remember, fear belongs in the passenger seat, never the driver's seat.

I will always believe the person addicted to drugs at the scene of the crime was a different person after years in prison. He taught himself Greek and Latin. He was quite educated and extremely well versed in the Bible. Even so, a complete change of heart and mind does not absolve us of the responsibilities of our actions. After writing to him, I got the feeling he felt the same way.

Have you ever found yourself in a place of extreme regret? Or regret but maybe not extreme? You've done something wrong or hurtful to someone else. No way to undo what has been done. I found myself feeling the pain this man may have felt. Found myself wanting to be conscious of the *Value Box* when the *Ego Box* has been exceedingly reckless.

"We learn a lot when we show mercy. We learn a *lot more* when we are shown mercy." -*Anonymous*

Norrell, it's time to tell the story.

Two people with little in common, met in a peculiar way. They became good friends. As time went on, they discovered they had much in common. Let me tell you about Norrell.

Finding myself less and less impressed with the material world and what can be viewed and judged with the eye, I started communicating with some people who were in prison. Assuming myself to be privileged and free. Whether we are incarcerated or not, I find a common thread among all. We are begging people to see past the folly and shame of our exterior. Pleading to not be seen or judged with the eye but judged with the heart. Every person is more than their worst moment, or their best moment for that matter.

Norrell, and I have never met in person, but he is one of my best friends. Anxious to help people and connect with them, I stumbled onto his acquaintance. Our connection was not a coincidence. We connected through *snail mail.* Reading some writings on a website written by prisoners, one especially caught my eye, written by Norrell. The text was an observation about societal ills and this materialistic world among other things. I have forgotten the exact details, but I penned a letter to Rel which was an eye-opener.

Rel had written an essay and it was published on this website along with other writings and articles from prisoners. He had deliberately only included text, no pictures. A picture of an author would be distracting. You would know their gender, race and judge by a few other characteristics perhaps. All this bias would filter what was written on the page. When we read only the text in front of us, our minds meet the writer on a more personal mental *playing field*, void of what our eyes would contribute to the conversation. The more we conversed, the more I found myself a prisoner wanting to be set free. Free from perceiving people from an external viewpoint, curious about what's happening on their inside.

We wrote back and forth for more than a year around 2006-2007. His street smarts came from Jamaica Queens, New York! I found Rel to be a true gift. Rel knows people, I mean knows how to read people. Has an uncanny feel for what people are hungry for and desperately need inside. He has almost five thousand friends on Facebook, a platform he uses the least. Rel is a teacher at heart, a teacher of the important things and it shows.

Something just now clicked with me about reading books. I can always get into reading a book, but isn't reading somewhat to learn more about the mind of the writer? Not solely to follow the storyline. Most books have a professional picture of the author somewhere on the cover. We look at the picture and pass judgment, it's a starting place. We can't wait to start reading and discover who this person is. No matter what the content is about you are going to learn about the author. An autobiography would tell us the physical details of an author, but the style and nuances paint a picture of the writer's mind. For example, one of my favorite authors is Mark Twain. I've read most of his books, short stories and articles. The subjects are varied, nonautobiographical, yet I get a *real feel* for how his mind worked. If we met on the street we could talk as if we'd known each other for years, even though clearly, we'd be strangers. Strange but true story, Norrell and I experienced this through *snail mail.*

My friend has an exceptional gift for conveying his thoughts. Has an easy way with conversation. A book reader, with hundreds maybe thousands of books to his credit. An empathetic soul. A gentle soul. Rel has a book inside of him I hope he publishes someday, maybe he'll have a few paragraphs about me. Fun fact about Norrell, he also helped me a lot with the self-care thing. More on this later.

Our story is one of the last pieces of this book. I came up against a *writer's block*. The gears just wouldn't start turning. I know what our friendship means but couldn't seem to get it on paper. When the storyline of this book began to develop in my head, I imagined a theme, the content and some supporting stories. Norrell's story would take up some space because it's important to me. Why was there such a mental roadblock about my friend? So, I got up in the attic and found a bundle of letters from Norrell, written in 2006-07. I discovered why I couldn't write. Looking over these old letters was exactly what I needed to start writing from a place of clarity and courage.

You see, it's not *time to tell the story* because this is where I want it placed in the book. It's time to tell the story because people should know the reality and power of understanding another person's value and worth.

Differences naturally generate alarm. We become uncomfortable and defensive when we sense a deviation from the *norm* we picture in our mind. It would be easier to get out of our comfort zone, except we have built walls which tend to keep us in. Furthermore, we place labels on everything we see and experience, stifling exploration, curiosity and openness towards what or who is different. Norrell wrote this: *We slap a label on people, look at the label, but never read the ingredients!* So frightfully true, how easy it is to get tripped up with a label and never take the time to dig and see what is truly inside of people.

What a stark contrast these two friends are.

Geographically, socially, racially, in so many *Ego Box* ways we are different. We talk on the phone or text like the good friends we are. Have our differences changed? No. Do they matter? No. Our skin color hasn't changed. For a long time, we didn't know for sure which color of skin the other one had. This color blindness was partly responsible for our keen friendship. Blindness, ironically, can give us a clear vision of the deeper side of people. I have tremendous respect for Norrell. His *Oregon trail* journey has given him a unique viewpoint as mine also has. He grew up on the *rough side* of town. Did he choose this? Would this influence his world view? Rel fought his way through life, and this gave him an education I couldn't begin to imagine.

How about me and my *Oregon trail* vantage point? There have been a few bumps, but I mostly got to ride in the wagon. Always had a place to sleep, plenty to eat. Did I choose this? Would this influence my world view? How can these dissimilar worlds meet? Meet on the grounds of mutual appreciation, love and genuine esteem. It will be difficult at best from a place of *Ego*, but it can happen from a place of *Value*. Rel and I are best friends because we appreciate each other's value.

What are the *building blocks* of great friendships? Growing up in the same neighborhood? Commonalities, like age, ethnicity, similar struggles? Or the same circle of friends? What can you add here? What is the glue that binds good friends together?

Well what differences generally wouldn't foster good friendships? Distance, incarceration, racial origins, age, neighborhoods, different circles of friends just to name a few. The few things we share in common are an interest in helping people and we're both nerds. Technology nerds, word nerds, information nerds. In this area we totally relate.

When I started reading those old letters, I was astonished to find out the beginnings of this book had already been written. Our conversation in those letters expressed astonishment at even meeting each other. I'm noticing the theme of much of our correspondence parallels the content of this book. I'm speechless, but not speechless enough to stop writing! What are the odds that two people with little or nothing in common could establish a deep friendship with only the power of pen and mind?

So far, I haven't had the slightest intention to write another book, this one has been quite the surprise to me in the first place. If I write another book it needs to be more about the unlikely friendship of Norrell. Here is a definition of faith: *It's like being on a team, but you don't know who all the players are.* This definition feels like the connection of Norrell and I, and others we meet on the journey.

If we follow the news, it would be so easy to throw our hands up, assume the worst in people and hide under the bed. Look at how much information is at our fingertips these days. Unprecedented. People in the free world are inundated with perspectives and viewpoints. No shortage of someone giving you a piece of their mind. We are conditioned to use someone else's mind, not our own. Many years ago, I tended to see the worst in people. We tend to keep ourselves closed up in a box. Have you ever built walls for fear of what was on the other side? If we continue to see the worst, it will never bring out our best.

You could say one should be careful when reaching out to people in this manner. Do you mean Norrell or me? Which one should be careful? It is true I could try to reach out to hundreds and hundreds of the prison population and never produce the same results. It's true, some care should be taken. Same with Norrell, he should be especially careful when talking to strangers. How many places and people would he need to search? Way too many. The time and place and person just happened to be right.

I have a dream that one day Rel and I would get together on a stage or podcast or something and share our story on a more personal public level. Might just be a *pipe* dream, but nonetheless it's a dream.

Scale the prison walls of your mind. Loose the chains that bind. Sands of time will tell the tale of the freedom that you find.
-Anonymous

Chapter 9. How are you thinking?

Inclusion and diversity.

Many large companies have a department totally dedicated to inclusion and diversity. I think they are attempting to bring awareness to the *Value Box*. Dig deep, don't just scratch the surface here. Understanding it's okay for everyone's *Ego Box* to be different isn't the same thing as seeing the *Value Box.* Kudos for the counterculture efforts in this arena. It's a difficult cultural shift to accept people for who they are. I get this, but what if *the way you are* is toxic? Keep some discernment in your pocket if it's needed.

Anyway, whether the shift is in corporate culture or national culture, the shift will not come easily. The shift can come organically from people who recognize and practice inclusion and diversity. Maybe companies initiate this kind of department to give everyone permission to be more aware of its presence and mission. People feel included when you send them a strong Value Message, and a signal that it's ok to take up space on the planet.

Excluding people needs no special department or training. This hurtful behavior comes to us naturally. Everyone has a strong need to belong. It could be simply including them in your conversation. Your inclusion efforts will build trust. Trust will build relationships. Relationships will build community. Community circles back to belonging. This practice is holistic in every sense of the word. In all this *building,* people will never forget how you made them feel.

Inclusion is a touchy subject for me. I'm not offended

anymore when I feel excluded, but I notice very deeply when this happens. The pain is scorching. Everyone has their emotional hot buttons. For some it may be the sting of losing a game. Yet others sense deeply the humiliation of rejection or the embarrassment of missing a goal. This pain point sensitizes my appreciation for helping people feeling included.

When I was a child, some of my friends and I were making fun of another boy who was quite different from the rest of us. We excluded him from our circle, ran away from him and teased him. He was heartbroken. His older brother found out what we were doing and turned the tide! His brother could have scolded us, chased us away or beat us up. He did worse! Without one word, he taught us an indelible lesson. He picked up his little brother, put him on his lap, comforted him and hugged him tightly, turning his back to us cowardly urchins. This rejected little boy was loved and included into a circle that mattered, delivered from one that didn't.

"If serving is below you, leadership is beyond you." -*Anonymous*

Complimentary drinks!

Drinks will never give you compliments, but aren't you glad when people do? Kind remarks are refreshing. Be the *cup of cool water* someone is needing.

I was maybe in my twenties when I distinctly remember getting a compliment about something I had observed. I have gotten compliments before, but this time it was genuine and out of the blue. I pondered the conversation over and over in my mind for a long time and have never forgotten the kindness. The message was a spark, kindling a flame of self-awareness and purpose. A purpose to find meaningful ways to genuinely compliment others. After all, speaking this new language was both free and freeing! Kindness costs nothing but is worth everything.

Looking back from this pivotal happening, my previous communication technique was at the least defensive and guarded. Often getting a proactive dig in, a fun method for putting others down to lift myself up. A form of passive aggression.

Peer pressure and what others think of you is clearly a killer. The *Emperor's New Clothes* for example. So caustically powerful is this dynamic, people die every day as a result of such poison. We can both give and take in the peer pressure department and scarcely be aware of it.

We crave love and belonging. We'd give our eye teeth just to be accepted by our peers. Over time we see the shallowness of this, yet we are in awe of its power. To go against the grain of the crowd will mean certain death of our ego and comfort zone. When we aren't afraid of death, courage comes! This was told by a soldier who survived *D-Day and* applies to many situations we face.

Eye app reach ate chew.

No matter how you say it, just let people know you appreciate them! I made some cards with this saying on it (Eye app reach ate chew.) patterned after the game *Mad Gab* (Mattel) and handed them out occasionally. I was a bit shy about this, but I'm not shy about putting it in this book. It's here for all the world to see, no apologies expressed or implied. Shame on me for being so slow to share compliments. The following story is how this message came about.

I was talking with a guy, new to the transportation division where I worked. The small talk to get acquainted and find out which sports team the other person roots for? I wasn't clear about his role and just out of curiosity wanted to know what he was doing here and to learn more about him as a person. Of course, wanting to see if he had any value to offer me, hee hee. I found him equally curious about my role and just wanting to learn more about the company and culture. At the end of our conversation he just said, "I appreciate ya." Wow I was taken aback. He just casually said those words, the way southern people might say as a friendly gesture or something. No ulterior motive or anything, just a genuine compliment and a thank you for talking to me. I was stunted and didn't know what to say. Pondering this for some time, I became aware of how little of this language we hear daily at work. The Value Message here was unbelievably simple: *I appreciate you.*

I think of myself as a secure person. Typically, I don't need compliments or approval to keep me motivated. However, hearing such a casual compliment made me swoon! I didn't think I had been starving for a compliment. What was up here? We all got our paychecks on time, had good insurance benefits and worked with some super neat people. Yet why must approbation and appreciation be such a rare occurrence? Yeah, another entire book could be written, looking for the answer to that question. The answer isn't just in front of us, I think it's within us. Jason for example, the "I appreciate ya" guy decided he wasn't going to wait for company culture to *start the fire*. He took it upon himself to make people aware of their real value. The Value Message here: *You are more than simply what you can do for me.*

Another guy my wife worked with was ever so charming, I envy his persona. Funny thing is, he wasn't strikingly handsome, nor muscle bound. Always shaved his head bald, which I liked. This gave us common ground.

Yeah, my wife's coworkers used to muse about this guy being on a pin up or calendar. Do you know what made *Prince Charming* such a *Dreamboat*? Your name. He did have a calming personality which was endearing too, but he called everyone by their name. Yes, you meant enough to him that he took the effort to speak your name. This was sweet and the girls took notice. I tried this at work too. After six months I found out Becky's name was Cindy. Prince Charming, I am not.

Today I read the following quote. It's almost spooky how often the right words and right people cross our path at the right time.

"Appreciation is the purest vibration that exists on the planet today." *-Abraham Hicks*

The Essentials.

More about appreciation. Spread that stuff around like confetti! For the past few years, Covid has shook things up a bit. From the stock market to your local restaurant. Until then, I had never heard the term *Essential Workers.* We're certainly finding out who they are. It's like the whole societal value system is getting a good shake down. Before now, I took workers in the service industry for granted. Assuming I was entitled to this service. "Shesh, my burger doesn't have a pickle on it". Who is the loser behind the counter responsible for such negligence? Now I don't even care about the pickle, if my burger comes wrapped up and mostly warm, I'm happy. By the way, "Thanks for showing up and thanks for your service". How tragic so many people had to die so I would learn to be more appreciative.

Years ago, my cousin worked at a fast-food restaurant. He said, "Never be rude to the help". Those people don't get paid enough to tolerate much *guff* from the public. Are you angry about that missing pickle and want another burger? Believe me, you'll be getting more than an extra pickle on the remake!

Another cousin works as a bartender at a busy restaurant (Bloomington IL), like so many places just trying to keep the doors open in these perilous times. She finds her coworkers still underappreciated occasionally. You might hear about kids nowadays feeling entitled. *Kids nowadays* step aside. You want to see entitled? Look at the senior white crowd (oops, that's me). This is what Anna tells me. Not long ago a table of fifteen seniors racked up a $233.00 bill and were quite rude to the waitress. They left a generous one-dollar tip. Another patron sitting next to them gave the waitress $40 to apologize for this classy bunch. The Value Message here is quite shameful. Shame on me when I cause others to feel unappreciated and clueless about their value. Shame on me when I don't take the opportunity to appreciate people every single day.

I wish I could believe some long-lasting appreciation and more compensation will be coming to the undervalued service industry. I have my doubts.

The *essential worker* thing is a supply and demand scenario. The supply is low, and demand is high for good service workers. When the *demanding* isn't so great, the value of essential workers will return to normal. Which is mostly an unappreciated state. Why is this? Because we value people for what they can do for us (Ego Box), not for who they truly are (Value Box). I hope essential workers will take the time to explore their actual value and not be disappointed with the shallowness of the masses. For example, what if as an essential worker I became more aware of these two boxes, the *Value Box* and the *Ego Box*? If my *Ego Box* is less appreciated or getting *clobbered* by others I can see and understand this for what it is. My *Value Box* is not affected. My self-worth is not determined by the *Ego Box*. I'm reminded again about what Lisa Nichols says about likes. "Learn to like yourself so much that any 'Facebook' likes, are a bonus".

"There will always be someone who doesn't see your worth. Don't let it be you!" *-Lorri Faye* (Facebook page: Life Rhino with Lorri Faye)

Reward vs. Value.

I'm not shaming the reward system but let's examine it more closely. A dictionary definition for reward is:

A thing given in recognition of one's service, effort or achievement.

This is benign enough yet will always have the essence of a carrot on the end of a stick. Rewards come in many different flavors and favors. The list is long; Pay raise, paycheck, pat on the back, gold star at school, spiced chai latte. We can easily get addicted to rewards and be left with precious little deposited in our *value* bank account.

This definition of reward is for the *Ego Box* only. Not judging here, just clarifying. Let's add to the above definition: *A thing given in recognition of one's service, effort or achievement of the Ego Box.* We may get that Emmy Award, pay raise or promotion but do we feel valued? The reward truly might have cost us a lot of work, blood sweat or tears. Rewards can be a *Landmark* or represent years of hard work or sacrifice. You may be quite deserving of such winnings. Rewards may help *pay the bills* but will be weak if you are looking for an impact on your value and worth.

Value Box value vs. *Ego Box* value.

I want to clarify something about value. Isn't it okay to appreciate a skill set or talent that clearly belongs in the *Ego Box*? Absolutely, but see this value for what it is. It's called *Ego Box, value*. Many companies struggle in this area. As a manager I could honestly and truly appreciate your skill set. Your people skills, your hard skills and whatever else you bring *to town*. When these skills are valued, I call this *Ego Box value*. It's just value that originates from your *Ego Box*. Your *Ego Box* skills make money for whoever you work for. This is a simple business arrangement. It may even be a *Win/Win*. Your paycheck for example, is an appreciation for your services. An employer might reward employees with paychecks, bonuses or Christmas parties as an attempt to show how valuable employees are. Yet this doesn't mean employers see or understand your *Value Box value,* at all. It only means an employer appreciates the value or product produced by the *Ego Box*.

To see my employees beyond a number or a machine and value them as a real person is starting to see into the *Value Box value*. It's possible to not even appreciate them as an employee or being on the verge of firing them and still see their innate value and *Value Box*.

Right now, a lot of the world is watching the Olympics. Another good example of *Ego Box value.* Some of the most athletically talented individuals on the planet show up for this highly televised contest. Grace, strength and ability put to the test. We are mesmerized by what the *Ego Box* can do. Not kidding at all.

A message to the often over stressed athletes on all continents and of all ages: Hang out with people who challenge you to up your game with the *Ego Box*. Better yet, hang out with people who will never ever lose sight of your *Value Box* and real worth. Do not compromise in this area. Real awesome Gold Medals will tarnish, real awesome friends will not.

How about some *Ego Box* history? You can do a further web search on the *1904 St. Louis USA Olympics*. About half of the Marathon contestants made it to the finish line. Thanks to brutal heat and the dusty road, exhaustion took its toll. The winner, Thomas Hicks, was racked with stomach pains for the last 10 miles. He was fed eggs, strychnine and brandy. Apparently, drugs weren't an issue back then. Another runner was chased off the course by wild dogs.

George Eyser was quite the gymnast. He had a wooden leg but still won six medals. There was only one event for women, Archery. Was that the *good ole days* or what? You know what my grandpa used to say about the *good ole days*? "No thanks, not interested!"

Leadership.

A CEO talked about his employees and a mindset shift that happened. I don't know what the industry was. All salaries were raised to a minimum of seventy thousand dollars per year. After this was instituted, he said, "Our sales went completely through the roof". Yes, this raise was compensation for a skill set, which comes from the *Ego Box*. However, the CEO was sending a strong value message. A message about worth. A message about value beyond the *Ego Box*.

"Show me the money", you say. "Show me the math which proves this to be financially doable and I'll do it." Who wouldn't give a raise for such results? No. I cannot and no, you probably won't do it. Why not? No math or formula will show this to work every time. Why? Because it's a *work of faith* so to speak. Which came first, the sales or the raise? The raise! The CEO had absolutely no guarantee that sales would *explode*. None at all.

Maybe he was watching some YouTube videos or read a book on the *Abundance Mindset.* I don't know. I would venture to say his decision didn't seem smart to a lot of his staff. Unless they were some who got a raise! He had a vision and a message. It might not have even made much sense to him. His Value Message was about the worth of his employees and they heard it. *I appreciate you for who you are, not just for what I can get out of you.* Point people to their *Value Box* and true worth...results will follow.

Politicians should never be confused with leaders. Some politicians could indeed be leaders, but it's not a given. Political figures rally followers to support their agenda. Which means without the leader, the cause will soon fizzle out.

Leaders foster leadership qualities in their followers. So, in the event the leader isn't present, the work and mission still move forward. So much *real-world* data demonstrates what good leadership is or is not these days. Many thought leaders in this space can be found in the library or on the internet. Some favorites are listed on my website

www.thevaluemessage.com/inspiration/people-that-inspire-me.

You might know by now who my *go to guy* for leadership is. Simon Sinek at simonsinek.com. He is well known for his positive outlook and has a passion for Leadership, an inspiring visionary. This is the heading on Simon's website and captures his mindset so eloquently:

We imagine a world in which the vast majority of people wake up every day inspired, feel safe wherever they are and end the day fulfilled by the work they do. -*Simon Sinek*

If you don't have an immediate answer or picture in your mind about leadership, what it is and what it isn't, you should do some research. Why? Because everyone, especially you, are in a place of leadership every day. A great opportunity awaits! Just looking a stranger in the eye and saying, "Have a great day", is a leadership quality worth having. Walking through the factory or out on the floor with a message of thanks, is a Leadership quality worth having.

If I want more out of my people, I needn't look at them for solutions, I must look at *me* for solutions. "Me? I'm not the one with the problem." No, of course not, but maybe you are the one with the solution. Something can always be learned about Leadership and the skills it requires.

Emotional Intelligence Agency (EIA).

The term *Emotional Intelligence* (emotional quotient or EQ) was created in 1990 by two researchers, Peter Salavoy and John Mayer. This phrase started showing up in everyone's vocabulary. Why should Emotional Intelligence be important to you? Why do you need to know more about this substance, and will it move you closer to Einstein on the *Smart Scale*?

Where you find yourself on the *Smart Scale* doesn't determine or predict your professional success. Intelligence is helpful but isn't a reliable indicator for how well you can manage life and relationship challenges. *Common sense* has been a success measurement and source of humor for eons. Yet it's hard to wrap metrics around common sense and the standards are subject to opinion.

How well you can manage emotions, now this factor will determine much about your life skills and success ratio. So no matter who you are, no matter where you are on the *Smart Scale,* improving your Emotional Intelligence will help you look and feel smarter.

Three fundamentals to Emotional Intelligence are:

1. Awareness
2. Awareness
3. Awareness

Three more important items to keep in mind:

1. Management
2. Management
3. Management

I'm guessing you think I'm just wanting to fill space here. Not so. This list indeed is very foundational for Emotional Intelligence. Becoming more aware of yourself and others is rudimentary to both personal and emotional growth. Learning to manage your actions and reactions is another *heavyweight champ* in the EQ arena.

What are some indications of an emotionally intelligent person? Someone who embraces change, has a strong sense of self-awareness and demonstrates empathy. This person will also be curious to learn, show gratitude and live a reasonably balanced life. More could be added, check out this enlightening subject when you have time.

You will be in a great place to develop and grow your EQ if the struggle of your self-worth is behind you. Think of what else could grow and develop if your mind wasn't constantly battling the question of your value.

Abundance vs. Scarcity mindsets.

These two terms were coined by Stephen Covey in his famous book, *The Seven Habits of Highly Effective People.* Perhaps you have read this or another writing of Dr. Covey.

Covey, Stephen R. *The Seven Habits of Highly Effective People.* USA, Simon & Schuster, 1989.

Many a business consultant and life coach has *snagged* on these mindset examples and fleshed them out for further study. After all, your thought patterns can change the entire direction of your life. Fostering an abundance mindset can be transformational. The beauty of your mindset is, it's something you have control over. Mindsets can be explored and changed or not changed and not explored, lots of possibilities here.

An in-depth study of abundance vs. scarcity is far beyond the scope of this book but looking further into the subject is worth your time. When I first learned about the abundance mindset, my initial thought was, this must be some new trend. Not that anything from 1989 would be new. People with an abundance mindset have been around for centuries. Old Testament Caleb and Joshua for example. Abundance thinkers have been scarce, however, and no one knew how to label them. Guess they called it the *Caleb, Joshua mindset.* These two men were sent with ten of their peers to scout and spy out the promised land. Caleb and Joshua belayed an abundance mindset, declaring that they were well able to take the land and all its bounty. However, the scarcity mindset of the other ten men prevailed, exhibiting fear and apprehension about any possibility of such a forward move.

The word *scarcity* seems dated to me. Like something *old school* or a way of thinking from the depression era. Yet scarcity mindsets have shown up in every generation and all situations too. These two mindsets show no consistency with circumstance or economics in my opinion. Luckily, we just happen to be living in a day when a plethora of information exists about how we choose to think.

How do we cultivate the power of an abundance mindset? Or steer away from the scarcity mindset? The choice should be quite clear, but let's gander at each way of thinking. I'm not trying to suggest how you should think. I'm suggesting that you can control how you think, more than you think.

Abundant mindset:

1. Openness to learn
2. Practice gratitude
3. Be conscious of the power of words
4. Develop a growth mindset
5. Be mindful of the power of thoughts
6. Cultivate your purpose and passion
7. You control how you react

Scarcity mindset:

1. Obsession with lack of something
2. Don't allow yourself to dream
3. Don't set bodacious goals
4. Unclear on opportunities
5. Fearful of lack
6. Others control how you react

This list is just scratching the surface. My intention is to bring mindfulness to these mindsets. Be more conscious about your thinking patterns.

Chapter 10. Real love runs deep.

Love and belonging spells value!

Approval from the crowd can lull us to sleep. It feels so warm and fuzzy! If we are famous, crowd approval can cause you to feel powerful, or it can derail your life. If you are average like most, this *feel-good* feeling just feels good and can inflate our confidence. Tread carefully here. Don't assume approval and acceptance from your peers means they clearly see and understand your value. They could simply be focused on your *Ego Box*, nothing more, nothing less. Time and experience will reveal your true friends and what they see. Relationships will either be a gift or a lesson.

Everyone seeks love and belonging, but don't just settle for *any ole love and belonging!* Look for the real thing. The mafia, drug dealers, stealers, the Pittsburgh Steelers and car dealers all know the power of love and belonging.

Brené Brown at brenebrown.com says, "In the absence of love and belonging there will be suffering." She referred to this as a "God Truth." You should write that down, it's rock-solid. I mean what problem in the world wouldn't more love and belonging solve? When we truly feel included, loved and have a sense of belonging, we will be getting a strong, positive and accurate message about our value. Don't forget, genuineness and authenticity must be along for the ride as well. Otherwise, it will feel like strings are attached and you will hear a distinct hollow sound.

Whenever I watch the Toy Story movies, this *God Truth*

comes to mind. "In the absence of love and belonging there will be suffering". The *suffering* makes good movies better. The *love and belonging* part is what people crave and connect with. Suffering is what happens when Woody and his friends aren't together or are rejected by the children who own them.

We all love approval. It does feel good but how good is it? No wonder we like it. The feeling we get is so cozy, but beware. We can be manipulated and rocked into a deep sleep by the approval of others. All conspiracy theories develop in this space.

Speaking of space, the Space Shuttle needs over seven million pounds of thrust to escape earth's gravitational pull. Attaining a speed of seven miles per second. Wow! How powerful is our need to belong? So powerful, that to pull away from the manipulation and approval of others will take force comparable to a rocket ship leaving earth! However, the result is freedom! Freedom from the gravitational pull of crowd approval!

The Golden ring.

When I was a kid, there was a gold ring with a diamond studded horseshoe shaped face in most jewelry stores. For some reason I got fixated on this jewel. Completely out of my price range, which was about six dollars, this didn't stop me from fantasizing about the clout such a nugget would bring me. Oh, how my life would change when my classmates and bullies viewed with admiration and envy such a life changing token on my finger. At the time I was such a loser. Didn't have popular clothes or shoes. I had crooked teeth and no muscles to show off. This one ring could tip the scales in my favor though. But such glory and power cost money I didn't even have, what a painful reality.

One day my uncle started wearing my ring, yep, the exact one I had been eyeing for months. Had he read my mind? Uh oh, what else did he read about my mind? After watching him for a few days, the ring didn't seem to change him at all. His problems didn't disappear. Everyone wasn't suddenly falling at his feet, as far as I noticed. I admired him, but no more or less with the ring on. This seemed strange. I mulled this over for a long time, what had I missed. Though perplexed by this distress I still clung to the fact that if the ring were on my own finger, magic would happen. I was always too embarrassed to ask my uncle to try the ring on, and only having six dollars kept me in a perpetual state of *Oh, what might have been.*

Dissect Approval, enjoy it, bask in it. Let it be your friend, not your enemy! Why do we crave approval? Maybe our own value is starving, hungry to be noticed and validated. How are we when it comes to disapproval? This is a good question to ask ourselves. When you sense disapproval, don't panic. Take a deep breath, drink plenty of fluids and call me in the morning! Our reaction to approval or disapproval, like a child with a garden hose, should be closely monitored!

Believe nothing about what you hear, and only half of what you see!

Our senses are just the coolest invention ever. They however aren't always reliable. We must be vigilant to be sure the data we receive is always accurate. For example, just the other day my wife and I heard it raining. Or was it water leaking somewhere? It was zero degrees outside, and a blue sky. So, rain seemed a bit odd, considering this. Hmmm, come to find out, rain was the background noise on the *calming music* video our daughter had turned on for us. Our senses were giving us information (data), but we had to do some fact checking before arriving at the truth (accuracy).

Like the rain example, ears can easily trick us. He heard her say, "Honey, what's for dinner?" Yes, she did say, "Honey what's for dinner?" What she said was, "Let's go out to eat." What the mind giveth, the ear taketh away!

Our eyes are the worst at trickery. Our eyes become so enchanted with the *Ego Box* they do not see the *Value Box*. Perhaps we would all be more spiritual if we were blind. Our senses would be more in tune with other people on a deeper level of understanding. Our *Spiritual Spidey Sense* would be stronger as we exercised this more.

I heard about a blind child, her family job was folding the laundry and separating it by owner. Even after the laundry was cleaned, she could tell who it belonged to by scent. Another sense had become more sensitive because the eyes couldn't be relied on. Our eyes think they are so great at accuracy. "I saw it with my own two eyes." How many times has that been said in the history of the world? The eyes are good for the three common dimensions of width, height and depth but other dimensions should be considered. The dimension of reality and truth.

It seems to me the *big Black Book* mentions a lot about the danger of appearing outwardly acceptable but inwardly despicable! What we can see with our eye about people will almost always pertain to the *Ego Box*. If people appear or behave a certain way, then we accept them. Accept them into our circle. Acceptance is not the same as love and belonging. Acceptance can feel like love and belonging, but it is not! Acceptance can be manipulative. Love and belonging are not.

I want to write about this subject because it is seriously dangerous to imply that just because you are accepted and approved by me and what I see, means what you are doing is all right. It is dangerous to give people the impression of love and belonging as a means of keeping them in your circle. It takes a strong constitution to examine ourselves in this matter, we might be guilty of doing this. Many cannot *stomach* the *heart* work of self-examination; myself included. It's so much easier to examine others and know exactly what they should be doing!

Judgment, hmmm.

A few years ago, it became clear to me that *my* judgment was off its rocker. Before this I had thought my situational perception was *on the mark*. As I looked back, I realized my judgment had a terrible track record and was quite inaccurate. Eventually I had to give it up altogether. I find this to be a work of progress. Old habits die hard. If we can leave judgment behind, a whole new world will open up to us. Discernment is a better option.

Discernment is defined as, *Perception in the absence of judgment with a view to obtaining spiritual guidance and understanding.*

I like where that's going. Not only was my judgment often faulty, but I also found out it wasn't even in my job description. If you can't look back at your life and see that sometimes you were an idiot, you're probably still an idiot! This could include how we perceive and judge people.

Everything is okay as long as *we* see it that way.

About twenty years ago some friends of mine and I were visiting some other friends. This was in southwest Chicago. Kind of a rough neighborhood. We always locked the car and parked it under a streetlight. We tried to avoid being there at night in the first place.

One time while visiting there, we heard distinct automatic gun fire less than a block away. An older lady who was with us exclaimed, "What was that?" Clearly alarmed, her eyes bugged out like dinner plates. One of the kids there said, "Oh, just someone working on their car" in a relaxed tone. "Oh, whew, what a relief", said the lady. Yeah right, ol' *Gomer Pile*, just trying to get a muffler off with his hammer!

Without a doubt that was automatic gun fire. I could tell by the number of police cars cruising the block and looking around everywhere. But everything was just fine with our lady friend if she could see the noise as someone working on a car. Does that make sense? I mean about what I'm trying to say. I know gunfire interpreted as car problems doesn't make sense.

I'm just saying, it's far too easy for us to have a warm fuzzy feeling about a situation because it looks and feels good in our own mind. Even though the truth and reality of said situation is so different from how we see it. Or how we choose to see it.

When people are not clear about their own value, they can unknowingly and easily be guided by crowd approval. We, unknowingly and easily cause people to focus on the *Ego Box,* which leads to people pleasing and a false sense of being valued. If we are overly concerned about how the crowd thinks, the part of our brain that does its own thinking will become numb and eventually go to sleep.

This is not to say we aren't aware of negative behavior, or we excuse people from being responsible for their behavior. For example, if your best friend is stealing from you, yes, he will soon be out of your *acceptance circle.* Will he feel pressured to conform and change this behavior? Hopefully. Can you control his behavior? No. Can he control his behavior? Yes. Be clear on this. Has his *Value Box* changed? Not at all. Has his *Ego Box* changed? Yes. The *Ego Box* now has a new label stuck on it. It reads *THIEF.* This would be an excellent place to set boundaries and not become an enabler by excusing such behavior. Being aware of your own value will help you a bunch here. Boundaries honor and establish your value.

However, if you are also stealing from your friend, I would mark this page and put this book down. Then go to your web browser and look up The *Law of Attraction.* The essence of which is, you attract what you are. Study that for a while then come back to this page.

The Power Tie!

Another example regarding crowd approval is the power tie. The power tie is a strong message. It's like having your own personal *National flag.* "This is who I am and what I represent". For instance, the President is clear on this. Politicians know about this for sure. I don't see women wear ties. I wonder what their *flag* is. Shoes perhaps? I'm not sure about the shoe thing, but let's talk about the tie. I searched for *Power Tie* on the internet. Wow! Now there's a lot of information to read through.

The tie you choose will send a message. That might be hard to believe, or that this is communication at all might be hard to grasp. Go ahead and search this on the internet. I dare you!

Is this a form of passive aggression? You know, you are sending a message on the sly because it's difficult to communicate openly. Or is it multitasking? I can communicate with my tie and body language and my mouth at the same time! This is largely cultural and just an observation. I'm guessing all cultures have a *Power Tie* of some sort. What message does *not* wearing a tie send? Observe high profile people who don't need to wear a tie and you will find people who are secure about who they are.

Years ago, a friend of mine managed a discount shoe

store. He was classy in appearance but from the hills of Kentucky. I remember the account of his first visit to the corporate office. Everyone had a suit and tie. Everyone was busy and distracted finding out which tie the boss would be wearing. This seemed to be the most important item on the agenda. My friend wasn't willing to spend energy on people who *ain't* from Kentucky. As you can imagine, yet more energy was wasted with the upset when my friend's tie didn't match all the others.

What you wear might be important, but only to you. What you wear only pertains to the *Ego Box*, never the *Value Box*. Does what we wear impact other people? Our attire sends a message, but how does it truly impact people? How we react to what people wear also sends a message about our shallowness or depth in this area. We put on those new shoes to feel good about ourselves. We dress up for a shot of dopamine. It feels good when we or other people like what we wear. The Value Message here: *If I'm enchanted with attire, I'm just looking at your Ego Box, dig those groovy threads!*

What it's like to like likes.

Lisa Nichols at motivatingthemasses.com says, "You need to like yourself so much that when you get up in the morning, you will be ok even if you don't get any Facebook likes all day." Can you hear the Value Message? Close your eyes and think about how much your life has been guided and baited by approval or disapproval of other people. The more you like yourself, the more firmly your feet will grip solid earth, I promise. Genuineness and authenticity will make this a smoother ride. Put differently, you need to like yourself so much that you begin to see your own value and worth even if others don't.

"When you are wanted, your ego is fed. When you are valued, your soul is fed." *-Lorri Faye* (Facebook page: Life Rhino with Lorri Faye)

If we don't like ourselves, we are already defensive. Maybe thinking no one else likes us either. Our default attitude may look like this: "I'll do what I want, when I want, no matter what I want.

I don't care what people think or say." You are completely free to chant this mantra. Let me know how that works for you and how many good solid relationships develop here. It's not at all what I'm talking about. That conduct is the spoiled child in us who will never be satisfied or happy. This is a zero-growth state which will imprison all who don't leave the compound. How enjoyable is the company of someone who has never learned to accept the word *no*?

We've all been in a place of pure frustration when everyone has some sage advice for us. Especially when everyone except us knows what our next step should be. Right? Often a "I will do what I want", is a *knee jerk* reaction when we are pressured. We lash out and send a message that we need some space here, *please step back to the line!*

When you are angry and they are angry, it's time to pick up your crayons and go home. It's not time to go home angry, it's just time to go home because the conversation is over. Don't spend energy here. "Were you born in a barn"? How many times did I hear this when I was a kid! The door is open, and energy is being wasted. The *door to communication is closed* but energy is still being wasted.

You could seek out only the people who appreciate you for who you are. However, you might find yourself hanging out with your grandparents most of the time! I say this because there's a better answer. Become more aware of *approval power* and its strong grip. Be more aware of your value and you will find yourself less defensive. The less defensive you are, the easier it will be to build relationships. Listening will be easier. You will be able to choose what you want, when you want, from a place of reason and wisdom. You will be better equipped to handle differences of opinion.

Right now, you may be making choices as a display of rebellion or spite. Or maybe from a place of surviving not thriving. Perhaps you will find people on your side more than you think. Maybe they just don't know how to be on your side. Most everyone else is wrestling with life too, no matter how strong and confident they seem. You could help them by learning to set boundaries. Setting boundaries is a skill set worth learning. The sanity it saves may be your own!

Everyone around us acts out of love or fear. Ourselves included. It is often difficult to tell whether it's love or fear. I implore you to take a deep breath, find your place of peace and step into the room with all the grace and courage you possess!

Keep fear fastened securely in the passenger seat. In due time, your navigation skills will improve, and you will be able to find your way around any obstacle. The Value Message here is: *Give yourself a big hug, everything is going to be okay.*
"Time doesn't heal emotional pain, you need to learn to let it go."
-Unknown

Atta boy!

The more aware we become of our innate value, the less we will be confused about crowd approval or lack thereof. Our craving for the Dopamine high that comes from crowd approval will lessen. You will get better at deciphering the motive and *genuineness level* of approval that comes your way.

Approval or disapproval is especially a challenge in our teens. Mom and Dad unwittingly helped me in this department. Neither one burned too many calories worrying about what other people thought of them. Maybe being a guy helps too. Just look at the shoes I wore back then or the cars we drove. We didn't have the money to worry about what everyone else thought.

As an example, I watched a TEDx talk not long ago. An ex-prisoner shared his story of recovery from drug addiction. He found himself doing two stints in prison as a result of his addiction. The change for him, happened when he realized he was available the least when his family needed him the most. Quite a remarkable story, he went on to get his master's degree in social work and has proven himself to be influential in the community, a model citizen and a true hero to anyone who knows him.

What caught my attention about his story was his observation of a new addiction when he was in college. Approval, he found himself addicted to *approval.* Dopamine is involved here! He asked his advisor one day about a course of action he could take. The advisor's casual unimpressed reaction was sort of a mystery to him. It was like the advisor's answer lacked enthusiasm, an over the top *Yippee* and congratulatory back patting! What he realized was this *lame* professor's answer and attitude was empowering. The way he answered implied no approval was needed, the ability and choice is not up to your professor or peers. Capability is within you. Kudos to the professor for conveying this message. The Value Message for this guy: *"You da man"! Courage and greatness come from within, not from without.*

"If you don't approve of yourself while others do, this may build resentment. By your words or actions, you will sabotage others' favorable impression of you." *-Anonymous*

Chapter 11. You don't know what you're made of!

The Belinda Chronicle.

Predators are experts at finding victims. It's like a sixth sense, unfortunately. How do you instill a sense of confidence or what else it takes in people to prevent this? We'd all like to know the answer to that question. We teach people how to treat us by what we tolerate, but too often it takes a long time to learn this truth and develop the skill.

Let's talk about confidence. This brings me again to Sheridan Elementary school in Bloomington, Illinois. I remember a girl named Belinda. She was a grade or two older than me and I mostly remember her while riding on the bus. Belinda exhibited confidence like no one I've seen before or since. When I need confidence or courage, secretly I attempt to put my *Belinda* face on and step up to the plate. This girl was average height and build, attractive, but her strong suit for sure was an unmistakable aura of confidence. She communicated this well, no words needed.

No one misbehaved on our school bus thanks to the driver, whose name was Wes. He looked like Don King except more muscles and a six-inch knife on his belt. It was in a sheath but quite in reach and we didn't want to find out how good he was with it. Us boys were thinking, "As a matter of fact I was just wanting to sit my butt down in the seat, keep my hands to myself and shut my mouth"! So, all the entertainment the kids were left with was the *gauntlet.* You know, the ritual of poking fun at and casting smart aleck remarks to little kids as they got off the bus.

Girls especially were subject to this tirade.

Except Belinda. When she got off the bus, the ritual was entirely different. All the boys closed their mouths and any stray thoughts just to be safe. To be even safer, they looked out the window at some distant interest or fumbled with their homework to be sure they hadn't forgotten anything important. Some even started to sweat, thinking of her older boyfriends sneaking into their bedrooms at night and cutting some fingers off. As far as I know no fingers were cut off, but maybe I just never heard about it. Like anyone was going to admit to such a thing.

She didn't have to kick or hit or say mean things to get off the bus. Her look got her off the bus. I remember her picking up all her belongings and just simply walking off the bus. Her eyes casually darting to and fro ready to cut the liver out of any opposition. Which boy was going to be so foolish as to even think something he shouldn't? Wes and his knife were not the ones to be feared here. Humiliation and embarrassment as this girl literally dragged you off the bus and beat you with a lead pipe, that's what was feared. Or worse yet she would say some snide remark and embarrass the offender in front of his friends. Belinda was good at teaching other kids how to treat her. The Value Message here: *If you value your life, value my life.*

Wynonna Judd sings a song titled: *One man woman.* The lyrics exhibit confidence because she is clear about what she is looking for.

"I'm a one-man woman looking for a one-woman man. If he ain't true and steady, then he ain't in my plans!"

No emotion or heartbreak drama. She is extremely clear on what she's looking for, her boundaries will not be moving, and compromise is not up for discussion at this time. This isn't a statement about morality. It's an example of confidence. Just saying.

Potential *come forth.*

Like a *taser,* you have a *stunning* amount of potential! What a fun subject potential is! Potential is sort of like a catapult when it's set. Stored energy is just waiting to be triggered. Here's my analogy for you! Until you pull the handle, there's no way to know how much potential you have. Look at all the viral YouTube videos giving witness to this truth. Rescues. Stunts. Close calls. Endurance and scary things, just to start the list.

Take the time to reflect here. Think of a time you were challenged and thought you couldn't do it. If you made it through, what helped you? Where did some of the help come from that you didn't see coming? Was there a pivotal moment when your feet hit the ground and you said, "No matter what"? You found courage and potential that wasn't there before.

One of my favorite *kids now-a-days* stories is on such a list. By the way, *kids now-a-days* are amazing if you haven't noticed. When I was young, kids were more average and mediocre. Except my neighbor friend, who lived down the street. He could swallow air and burp at will for an embarrassing amount of time. It's all relative but we figured he was the coolest kid on the planet!

Yeah, this video is good. On a hot summer day some boys are weaving in and out of cars in a parking lot on their skateboards. What? Why can't they be at home texting or playing video games like other kids? Their *unreasonable* parents just made them get out of the house or something.

Suddenly one of the boys sees a child locked in a vehicle. Immediately he tries to smash the window with his skateboard. This does not work. Tempered glass is not easily broken except in the movies. A crowd starts to gather, taking video and pictures. Someone calls 911. Suspense builds, I'm on the edge of my chair. Dude, seconds are ticking away.

Luckily, Hercules was on scene and grabs a concrete parking post out of the ground and rams it through the window. When concrete post speaks... window listens! The glass is cleared, someone opens the door and gets this hot sweaty kid out and cooled down. You know what kids do *now-a-days*? They save lives. Yes, that's right, they save people's lives. Talk about being at the right place at the right time. It was literally minutes away from a tragedy.

Let me say more before we get to the value lesson. I would love to meet the boy who first started to break the window. His courage and quick action were truly heroic. I just picture my cowardly side in the same scenario. It could have gone something like this… "Oh, no there's a kid in the car. Oh, I don't want to get involved or make a scene. Someone else should be doing this. Not my job. People think I'm just a no-account skateboarder anyway, they'll think worse of me if I start tearing up this car. Wow that car looks expensive, I don't want to scratch it. I just don't know what to do, so guess I'll just do nothing".

If you watch the video, not the remotest hint of such dialogue appears. Not the slightest. This young man took immediate action with the tools he had in hand. This drew a crowd and utilized resources. People made themselves available to help. An added bonus was Hercules being close at hand with the concrete post. This was the kind of kid who would've scratched the window until his fingers bled to help the little child, ya know. His action inspired more action. The Value Message to the hot tot was: *You are valuable, we don't care what it takes!*

Old Aunt Nellie.

Way out in the African bush a village's only source of water was a well a few miles out of town. Every day the chief and some villagers would load up in a grain truck and go get water, even Aunt Nellie. Auntie had to be helped up into the back of the truck. No easy matter, using a step stool and the aid of any able-bodied man who would help her slowly climb aboard.

One day while at the well, everyone was out of the truck filling containers with water and a lion showed up. The villagers scurried as fast as they could getting into the back of the truck to safety. Alarmed, the chief shouted, "Where's Old Aunt Nellie"? "She was the first one in the truck" someone exclaimed! "She knocked me down as she was climbing in", added another.

The moral of this story is: *Sometimes it takes a lion to find potential you didn't know you had!*

Chapter 12. Don't beat yourself up. Life will do it for you.

I gotta great idea! Yah, right.

In May of 2019 my wife and I decided I could quit my current job and babysit our two girls for the summer, ages five and six at the time. My wife's niece and nephew also spent a lot of time with us. *Daddy daycare* was now open for business! With a plethora of activities to do, the summer breezed by. The days were filled with lazily lollygagging at the local pool, jumping on the trampoline, ruining furniture with home-made slime projects, watching movies or doing fairly safe *hacks* posted on YouTube videos.

This was during the day. In the morning when everyone was sleeping, I was getting educated at YouTube University! Educated about anything that could keep our bank account from drying up! I watched hours of helpful information on YouTube about real estate, being a YouTuber, Life Coaching, Motivational speaking, tons of personal development stuff. Anything that could be a good fit for me. My nephew, who slept most of the day, was also a great resource as a YouTube genius. I picked his brain whenever I could find him awake.

At that time Life Coaching, Motivation and Personal Development was just a hobby of sorts. The time came when it was more of a lifeline, which made me an even bigger consumer of anything in the personal development space.

After soaking in lots of information about Real Estate and Financial Education, I now knew everything there was to know about these two subjects, so I thought! Especially enchanting were some thoughts about mistakes and education. The gist was: Don't be afraid of making mistakes, it's how we learn! Well, that was empowering for me, especially the first part about mistakes. "It's how we learn", I was soon to be educated about the magnitude of those words!

I'm a poor communicator and I do it well! I didn't tell anyone about a house soon to be auctioned off. Didn't even tell my wife. Showed up in the evening of the auction day. Mesmerized by this huge old Victorian era house I wondered if it would come close to my price point? The bidding came down to one other guy and me. When the tension was high, I asked to call my wife to help me decide... "sure take all the time you need", they said.

She was in a meeting and my phone call must have been a shock and a lot of pressure. Did I get the bid? Yes. Was my signature binding? Yes. We got the house, used all our savings for the down payment, had no job, had no money, had no sense and had some house payments to think about. As you would expect, there was considerable tension at the Sarver house for a while, both houses.

Unfortunately, I was learning a lot about myself. Fortunately, I also was learning a lot about other people. This literally blasted me out of my comfort zone, and I became painfully more self-aware. Aware of two things particularly. For one thing, I am an *avoider*. When conflict or problems arrive, I *make like a tree* and leave! Let someone else handle the *pain points*.

I also learned I'm *afraid of success*. When I was close to success, I would use self-sabotaging behavior because success was outside of my comfort zone. Failure brings sympathy and I don't have to be embarrassed by my lack of skills when I fail. I was a sympathy addict. This means it's just too easy to sabotage your projects in exchange for the dopamine hit, induced by a little sympathy. To be successful would mean a lot of stress, it's intimidating besides!

So, my wife, certainly not an avoider and not afraid of conflict, helped me learn a few new skills. My first plan after doing the math, was get a job and just pay the big yellow house off in three years. Nothing ventured, nothing gained. Or just give them the entire down payment and walk away, so easy and safe! The

Mrs. wasn't so keen on this idea! Go figure! In her clear straightforward communication style, she pointed me in a different direction!

Learning more about people was a bonus for me, people are truly amazing. Starting with a local dairy farmer and good friend, who hired me to feed the cute little cows for therapy and income.

I was so stressed., I didn't eat or sleep for about three days. Motivational speeches, affirmations, Life Coaching and personal development material were all that tasted good to me. I stuffed myself on this digital buffet until my strength returned and I could get out of bed and somehow dig myself out of this hole! *Adulting* wasn't something I was familiar with!

Somewhere in the timeframe of *inspirational speaker immersion* I started to see commonalities within their stories. Some of the most inspiring people on the planet have gone through some tough times. Wow... News Flash! Nobody born with a silver spoon is going to have an interesting story! This isn't new news, you already know this, but it was sort of new to me. Yes, I'm closer to the raccoon than Einstein on the *Smart Scale*! I wasn't born with a silver spoon, for sure, yet staying in my comfort zone would never help me grow or have a story to tell.

Steve Harvey for instance. I just thought he was the funny guy hosting *Family Feud.* He came from humble beginnings. Lived out of his car for over three years while he was trying to be recognized. Did you know he stuttered terribly as a child? Steve told his class he wanted to be on TV when he grew up. The teacher shamed him terribly, even reported the infraction to his parents. After Steve made *the Big Leagues*, he sent his teacher a brand-new TV every year. Because you can't watch TV without seeing Steve Harvey somewhere. I just love that guy. When you are down on your luck, you feel like he understands and has a message of hope for you personally.

Now to make a short story, long... Here is what happened with the big yellow house. We cleaned and painted everything inside. Painting it all white, it felt like a hospital. The previous owner was truly amazing, a kindly gentleman, kind of the *artsy* type and this added to the aura of the home. He was a contractor and had spent thirty years remodeling the house. Updated all the plumbing, electrical and HVAC. The home was well maintained, to my advantage.

When I had spare time, I would network. Because we always hear networking is such a good idea. On YouTube, I studied every good and bad thing about hosting with Airbnb and decided to try it. When the house and business were completely in place, I went to the local Chamber of Commerce to let them know I was in town and ready to be the *hostess with the mostest*.

Was I ever surprised when I met a man in the Chamber office, also new to town. He was searching for something! Searching for an Airbnb to rent for several months. This guy was a contractor and would be working on a job for about one year and needed a place to live. He was a seasoned Airbnb host himself and had a wealth of information to help me get started.

The whole *yellow house adventure* nearly *swamped my boat*. I was learning the truth of that familiar saying, "what doesn't kill you, makes you stronger". Except bears. Bears will definitely kill you!

What's in your toolbox?

Over the years your mental *toolbox* will accumulate tools which make your jobs and projects easier. It's good *housekeeping* to occasionally take an inventory of these tools. Some are useful and some are not. For example, without personal growth we will be apt to use only the tools we are familiar with. Even if these tools are ineffective, we'll use them again and again. Maybe it's whining or avoidance; the tool is in easy reach, and we know which drawer it's in. These impractical tools have *comfort zone* and *complacency* written all over them.

Cultivate a hunger for better and more tools. If you are a guy, you will identify strongly with the notion that *you can't have too many tools.* If you are a girl, think about shoes. *You can't have too many shoes.* Learning about useful tools is the gift that keeps on giving.

Three tools have been especially helpful to me; a good resource.

1. Journaling
2. Vision boarding
3. Affirmations

I would hope you'd find them useful as well. However, these are merely suggestions. Everyone learns and comprehends in different ways. A tool that works for you may be clumsy for me and vice versa. So, I am just going to give a brief overview of this tool set.

Journaling.

Tracking your thoughts and observations in a journal might not only be helpful but could reduce your stress. Writing down what's on your mind is therapeutic. When you write something down, it has a much greater chance of being acted upon. Whether it's things you think about or organizing your days and weeks, journaling may be one of most useful items in your toolbox.

May I recommend *Bullet Journaling,* at bulletjournal.com? The brain can quickly get cluttered and overloaded. Do your mind a favor and write down how you feel and what you think about. Sort it out after it's on paper. Your brain will thank you. I had no idea how much energy was expended using my head for the wrong job. Gray matter is better suited for problem solving, not data storage. Put your schedule, ideas, plans and parties on paper, get them out of your head and notice how the creative juices flow.

Bullet Journaling is a way of journaling developed by Ryder Carroll. Ryder's method is geared toward organizing your calendar, but the sky's the limit. You can apply this methodology to many areas of your life. Long and short-term plans, scheduling and dreaming will all look better in print. Your blood pressure may even drop a few points. You can use a simple notebook or buy a Bullet Journal ready to go from Ryder's website. Your day, week, month and year can be laid out at your fingertips. You'll be able to watch everything like a hawk, seeing your plans from a *Bird's*

Eye view.

Until a few years ago journaling wasn't even on my radar. I shudder to think where I'd be without this tool. Lots of people already employ this skill, I was surprised to find out. A quick internet search will give you lots of ideas. Change your mindset to work and think smarter, not harder! Like Einstein, not a raccoon!

Vision boarding!

Vision Boarding, much different than surf boarding, is a close cousin to *Bullet Journaling.* Creating a Vision Board also is a skill or theory to learn more about. A Vision Board will prove to be a well-worn tool, keep it shiny. A tool that helps your mind focus on something specific, the results might surprise you or someone else.

A Vision Board workshop is an excellent networking event. All you need are some willing participants, a large box of old magazines, some glue and some good chocolate! If you've done any research, you know there's lots of versatility in how a Vision Board is designed. Here is the way my Vision Board is constructed. It's only a starting point. Unleash your creativity!

1. Cut out a cardboard rectangle approximately 2 ft. x 3 ft.
2. Draw a grid on the cardboard 3 cells wide x 3 cells tall.
3. Cells should have plenty of space to paste a picture or write large words.
4. Decide on the theme or content in each cell.

Below is a drawing of the layout I use. You can customize this however you want or just stick to what is in the picture.

Vision Board

Wealth	Spiritual	Reputation
Relation-ships	Love	Health
Career/ Education	Hobbies	Travel/ Fulfillment

A helpful video can be found on my website or YouTube titled: How to create a vision board that works.
www.thevaluemessage.com/productivity/vision-boarding.

This video creator presents a straightforward process and explanation for using a Vision Board. I never heard of these until a few years ago.

As you place images or words on the board your brain begins to focus on these items and searches out opportunities you might not have been aware of otherwise. Are you wondering what exactly to place in each cell? Look for pictures or words that pertain to the cell topic. *Career/education* for example, write something reasonable and attainable to start with. Open your mind up to possibilities though. What do I mean by this? If you have drawn up your board with the grid and labeled each cell, your brain has already *snapped to attention.* Writing $100,000 per week, in the career cell might set you up for disappointment. $100 will be playing it safe. It's hard to describe but you start talking to your brain about the cell content like you would chat with your high school math teacher. The conversation might go something like this: "Well, $100 is ridiculous, but $100,000 is just totally nuts. What about $1,000? $2,000 feels exciting and on the edge. Let's just put down $2,500 and see what happens."

So, you see this inner dialogue starts taking place and you find yourself getting off the couch. Your energy level gets bumped up because you are suddenly empowered to plan some changes. Your mind is excited to get an overview of this new strategic dashboard, creativity is waking up and so is your belief in the power of your mind. It's no special magic. It's just helping your brain. You guessed it Einstein, work smarter not harder. By the way, don't write $2500. This must be a number you have arrived at, no one else! Your vision belongs to you alone.

Whether it's journaling or vision boarding, something powerful happens when information and messages get in front of you. Then your mind and eyes can collaborate with your feet and hands to expand your world! This brings us to another tool of honorable mention.

Affirmations.

Sounding out this word wasn't easy, let alone grasping a definition. It was a while before it dawned on me that the root word was *affirm.* Duh!

Similar to journaling and vision boarding, affirmations were another tool that proved exceedingly useful in one of my darkest hours. Trying my best to sound like Sir Winston Churchill.

Bob Baker at bobbakerinspiration.com is a good place to begin for affirmations. Bob has several videos on YouTube as well. He also has authored a book on this subject.

Baker, Bob. *The Power of Affirmations and Positive Self-Talk.* USA: Spotlight Publications, 2021.

Thousands of affirmation websites and videos are available. Some will be a better fit for you than others, but this is my offering for a place to start.

Affirmations are affirming statements that train your mind to focus in a certain direction. It's also under the category of *working smarter not harder.* Affirmations are a *broad-spectrum* product. Statements can be about health, wealth, finances, positive thinking and more. If you write a statement and stick it on your mirror to see and repeat every morning, this is an affirmation. Do this exercise, write on a piece of paper these words, "I am enough" or choose your own affirmation. Tape this on your mirror for two weeks, look at it more than once a day and say it out loud. Say it and listen closely. If this is a new practice for you, don't be surprised to notice movement in the right direction.

Audible affirmations are the equivalent of your grandma singing, "You are my sunshine, my only sunshine". Remember how good that made us feel? Everything was going to be alright. No, affirmations are more than grandma's steady voice and tender love. Both are positive messages that leave a tangible impact. Pick a positive phrase and repeat this to yourself or listen to a variety on the internet.

Some neuroscience is at work here and phrases needn't be complex. At first this may seem awkward, but time and practice will smooth the operation. Affirmations are repeated statements or phrases that use positivity to chase away negativity. "You are my sunshine. You are enough. You are amazing. You can do this". Find the ones you are needing that resonate with you, listen and relax.

Speak these words from a place of belief, not *wish!* Saying "I *do* have value" is different from, "I *have* value". "I do", could feel like you are trying to make a sale. Trying to convince or persuade your mind by repeating a statement. "I have value", is expressing a truth worthy of belief. An expression void of doubt.

Affirmations stood by me when I needed them the most. I've never forgotten this resource and its effectiveness. These days I sort of incorporate affirmations in my meditations. Sometimes uttering positive statements audibly, sometimes silently. This practice has helped me think soberly about the power of words. You know I love this subject because what are affirmations but simply messages. Positive and negative words have great energies and should be respected.

When you realize you are the gatekeeper in charge of the positive or negative flow, you will look for ways to open the positive gate wider. At some point you'll want to rip it off the hinges!

Life Coaching.

Life Coaching, personal development and motivational offerings can be a *Life Preserver!* When we put to practice what we hear and read, the ball starts rolling. Seeing your value and self-worth will take these *commodities* to a whole new level.

When I was learning how to be a *Life Coach*, I worked with a few clients, all of whom were quite capable with their affairs. In fact, it was difficult to know who was teaching and who was learning. The coaching classes I took were methodical, logical and chronological. Clients found this to be useful, even though I was a complete novice as a coach.

Life Coaching is a gift that keeps on giving. To learn and practice new life skills is laying a solid foundation to build on in the future. Investing in a Life Coach to help navigate some difficult terrain on your journey has a good ROI. Coaching can introduce you to new viewpoints or tools. The next time challenges come your way. You'll at least have an idea where to start. Confidence and resilience will increase as you'll have a better sense of what to do or not do. Having a plan, knowing your resources and taking action will develop your *empowerment* muscle.

Assess Your Value

If I work with clients again, I will only change one thing. The first thing I would do is assess where clients are with understanding their own value. A questionnaire might look something like this:

1. On a scale of 1-10 where do you see your value?
2. How clear are you on self-care?
3. Define the term, self-love.
4. On a scale of 1-10 how comfortable are you with being alone?
5. How difficult is approval or disapproval for you?

Imagine the following mindset.

1. You have a vision of your value and worth.
2. Your Ego and Value boxes stay separated.
3. Self-care is second nature for you, it comes easily.
4. You are comfortable with conversations about loving yourself.
5. It's okay for you to be alone.
6. Approval or disapproval is a navigable landscape for you.

The tool for you.

I've developed this highly non-technical illustration called: The Value Orientation Tool! The purpose is twofold.

1. Assessment of where we are regarding our value.
2. Assessment of where someone else might be in understanding their value.

Value Orientation Tool

☐ ☐ ☐ ☐ ☐ ☐ ☐ ☐ ☐ ☐
1   2   3   4   5   6   7   8   9   10

**Least
Value**

**Most
Value**

A person at the lower end of the scale (1) will not have clarity of their value. No judgment, this is a tool, not a test. The person on the higher end of this scale (10) will be a completely different person because they are aware of their value.

Let's say you honestly place yourself at 3 on the (VOT)

scale. What if, after reading this book you feel the understanding of your value is close to 9? Even though it needs to be at 10! Yes, the truth is you are a 10, no exceptions. Do you think this would just increase your knowledge alone? No, your capacity to set boundaries will have improved. Your view of other people will change. Self-confidence will develop. Growth will show up in other areas too. Take this assessment now. Record the results, retake after reading the book.

Originally the intent of the Value *Orientation Tool* was simply a conversation starter about personal value. A fun exercise at a workshop. As it turns out, this illustration isn't just a *talking point* but could be the focal point of this entire book.

If your mindset could get wrapped around your value, Life Coaching would get better *traction.* With this mindset whatever the next step is, your feet will be on firmer ground. Opening a business, expanding a business. Going through a difficult time, a divorce, bankruptcy or illness. Your next step might not be easy, but you will have the amperage to start the engine. You will have the courage to drive the car.

Why do so many of my metaphors have something to do with vehicles? Is it to convey forward motion? Or because I like to travel? Who knows? I don't hang my head and tongue out the window, but like my dog, I do love to ride in the car.

When we struggle with our worth and value, it's like a barking Chihuahua, constantly nipping at our heels. Can you picture this? Whatever goals and plans you are trying to accomplish, here comes that barking Chihuahua. When you are with people, or by yourself, here comes Mr. Yap Yap. You are trying to be a better person or trying to overcome an addiction. Here comes that annoying little doggie again with lots of energy and never sleeps! This yapping pooch is a *thorn in the flesh.* Visualize how your life would be different and more restful without it.

To further press the point, how often have you faced difficulties or started with a plan only to fizzle out a few miles down the road? Were you soon overwhelmed with self-loathing and doubt? Afraid of what other people thought? Afraid of what other people would think of your value? I'm not saying, if you are crystal clear on your value the road will be smooth. What I am saying is, some obstacles associated with not seeing your value and worth will no longer be in the way. Obstacles, not just easier to navigate around, obstacles that cease to exist.

"If people don't want to change, you can do very little or nothing to START them. If people want to change, you can do very little or nothing to STOP them!" -Anonymous

Chapter 13. A dark and stormy night.

It's a long way home.

When people see their own value and self-worth, the game will change! Countless tragic stories from the files of humanity could be told. Some of which are about well-known or famous people. Fame and fortune are not always your friends. Many famous people, more so the *young and famous,* find tremendous success and then the tables turn? Maturity and wisdom are needed for such circumstances.

Anyhoo, the story follows this common thread… said person starts a downward spiral of abuse. Either being abused or self-abused in one way or another. Anyone of us would falter under such pressure and duress, so certainly no judgment here. At some point there usually is a turnaround, things get better and sometimes the story has a happy ending. The common ground here is when this person starts to see their value and self-worth and can love themselves, things begin to change. Anne Hathaway is a prime example of such a life change. It's remarkable how much of a shift comes about when we are nicer to ourselves.

Don't just survive, thrive!

It was a dark and stormy night. So many stories start with this captivating theme. So many possibilities can come after this. So many tragedies take place on *dark and stormy nights*. Even if that night is only a struggle in the mind.

Self-harm such as suicide is not a subject to take lightly, but let's bring this to the table for some discussion. *Self-harm statistics are alarmingly on the rise, anyone reading this book likely knows someone related or close to you who has taken their life.* Annual suicide rates are 2.5 times the annual homicide rate. News just came to us a few days ago of another tragedy. Someone we used to work with ended their life. Rarely does this happen and we aren't surprised. Let's just assume everyone you meet needs a reason to face another day. Everyone can benefit from getting a positive message about their value. Thanks in advance for your compassion and kindness to someone who needed it the most. You will never know who that person is. Statistics can't show saved lives or thwarted attempts. Your message could open the door of hope for someone who supposed it to be tightly closed.

Does anyone need to hear a positive message about value instead of performance? The competitive pressure to perform among young athletes has been in the headlines lately. Rightfully so, parents and coaches share a deep concern about the many sources of stress students face. Pressure to perform, humiliation that comes with failure. Being unprepared for life's challenges. Pressure comes from your opponents but also from your peers. Often, it's easier to face the team you lost to, than your teammates in the locker room after the game.

Furthermore, student debt, stress about the uncertain future and adults asking so many probing questions can be daunting. Questions for which kids don't yet have answers. Everyone else seems to have their *ducks lined up. Why am I the only one on the planet feeling so down and out?* You know these exact or similar thoughts come to young people as they have to you. Kids have so much going for them, so much talent and so much incredible value. So strange, everyone can see this except them. If this person or young person is you, it would be a good time to trust people if they are trying to help you see your *Value Box*. These same people are trying to help you not take the *Ego Box* too seriously.

Bullying is a huge subject, too large for this book. The *power tripping* of bullying has cost many a life. This disgraceful behavior comes so naturally, it's a cultural hallmark. Seems like everyone is doing it now-a-days. At work or school, don't let a bully determine how you perceive your value! The seriousness of bullying is one reason this book is written. The insidious abusive act of bullying can annihilate the understanding of your value like nothing else. In one *fell swoop* you can doubt your worth, hate yourself and wish to die, seeing no escape from such searing pain. Bullying is a champion of carnage, it's a poisonous superpower on steroids.

William Shuttleworth graced our little town a few years ago. Such a pleasure to meet this guy. Some of the local Vets arranged a dinner with him at the Masonic Lodge. Mr. Shuttleworth was a 71-year-old Veteran walking across America. He was a grand presence with a great mission. Bringing attention to Veterans' needs and some areas of neglect. Elevated suicide rates among this populous are concerning. His journey lasted 110 days, took 5 pairs of shoes and spanned 3,300 miles. Thanks for your service, Mr. Shuttleworth.

Over the years, I have entertained thoughts of taking my life. This *train of thought* has sort of evolved. Evolved is the best way I can describe this strange journey. I wonder how many can relate. Have you struggled in this area? More importantly, what is the most effective way to help anyone on such a *dark and stormy night?*

In my struggles as a teenager, the thought of taking my life came from loneliness. When I was in this state of mind or stressed it was like one of six options to cope with a situation. The suicide option was just always one of many available. There was a time when I wanted to use this option for power, as a way of revenge or to gain attention. This was a time in my life when coping skills were minimal or non-existent. The fear of rejection and extreme loneliness were heavy struggles for me, and I didn't know who or how to ask for help. At the peak of this trauma, mostly self-inflicted, I was hospitalized. This was a disappointing venture from which I found little professionalism and even less tangible help. I am grateful however, for the concern of friends and family and the time to rest my mind.

The man I worked for at a print shop was empathetic and talked to me about my struggles. He was curious about my feelings, he never at all felt like taking his life for any reason. He never thought of it as an option ever. At the time I remember being shocked by this statement. Would that ever be possible for me? Sometimes my internal pain felt to me like my hand was on fire. What would you do? Extinguish it of course, this would be the only way to stop the agony.

In the hospital, I was asked a lot of questions but not one of them was about relationships. Relationships are a huge influence factor in our life and state of mental health, in case anyone didn't notice. Thanks to my control freak mentality, dreaded fear of loneliness and stress of the future, my relationships weren't going as planned. I was not equipped to maturely handle this challenge and it showed!

A door of hope!

A few years later I came across the mindset and writings of Dr. William Glasser at wglasser.com. His work was monumental to my personal development, and I connected with his message. *Control Theory* was the first of many Glasser books I read. I found answers and tools to help build relationships. His offering spelled out supportive details as to why relationships work or don't work. According to Dr. Glasser, we are all either control freaks or recovering control freaks, this reassuring truth became a guidepost.

The subject of taking your life is simply difficult to bring up. Alarm bells and panic set in for caregivers and parents, we feel so unequipped for this conversation. Like other situations as a responsible adult, we are at a loss of the next right thing to do. I don't pretend to have the answer, I just don't. However, I'm more and more convinced that speaking a Value Message and being mindful of this *Value Box* illustration is a firm step toward proactive prevention.

What does *proactive prevention* look like? You wouldn't believe how many people are scrambling for the answer to this question. I didn't believe it myself. My intention for discussing this topic was only a few paragraphs. After assessing so much feedback and concern from early book reviewers, I realized there might be an elephant on the table and a deeper purpose for the birth of *The Value Message*.

If we struggle with suicidal thoughts, most of the time we aren't the ones who are alarmed. It's just a curiosity kind of dialogue in our heads. Taking our life is a long-term solution to a short-term problem, yet it's so easy to get fixated on the short-term problem. If we aren't accustomed to using problem solving skills, our struggles will be magnified and appear larger than actual reality.

I would tell my younger self to, "Be patient, you have immense potential and value". I did have a lot of friends and family who conveyed that message for which I'm grateful. Instilling a sense of value in people is being proactive. This message could be spoken formally, like a presentation or motivational speech at school or your place of business. Or talking individually to *at-risk* students or acquaintances. Remember a Value Message can be spoken with or without words, be on the lookout for every opportunity.

Would a discussion about understanding my own value and potential have changed my outlook? Would I have been able to even receive such a message or concept? How do you feel about that question if you can relate? Hindsight is always so clear and when the stress is over, we fantasize about how much better it would have been *if only*. One thing I know for sure is you are absolutely worth the effort of such a discussion.

A Song of Hope.

Not long ago I became acquainted with a young man named Austin. He is a writer and poet. Writing ended up being a much-needed outlet for him. You can read one of his poems here. This writing captures his story very well. It's raw and it's real. Austin's struggle with self-harm came to a peak at the age of twenty-one. I love what helped him overcome such inclinations. He has written many poems since and clearly is an advocate for any who struggle with ending their life.

Austin's Poem

I know there's kids who look up to me
But I don't live my life so perfectly
So here's what happened to me
Just be ready for the lines you're about to read

Everything started at thirteen
I was the quiet kid
Afraid to speak up to the ones who bullied me
But never forgot what they did

Next year that followed
I started feeling hollow
Self hate started to form
Cause I got addicted to porn

I was just a kid who cried himself to sleep every night
I would think about how I would die
Cause I was losing this fight
So I figured the best way out was to commit suicide

Started feeling worthless
Just wanna slit my wrist
But I was too scared to do this
So I had to resist

Years went by with depression
But loneliness stepped in
Showing me there's no mission
For my life but someone else stepped in

Throughout my life family started slipping away
Some don't want anything to do with me anyway
Others lost their lives
And kids around my age never put down the knives

Wont forget the day I broke down
In the parking lot at twenty one

Staring at the ground
Searching through every thought
To keep going on
So I let it out with a single post
Now everyone wanna listen
But I cried when I saw what they wrote

Family started finding out
But what kept me going were the kids crying and praying for me
That's something I just can't unsee
Cause I heard they looked up to me

I couldn't go through with this anymore
I don't want them taking the same path
Had to remove all pain and regrets I wore
Now here comes the aftermath

Went to therapy
But that didn't work for me
Cause I held everything back
That's just me
Controlled by insecurity

To this day I still fight a few enemies
But I fight them differently
Moving forward with my life
Now at twenty three never wanna end my life

Music was the only way out
I wont forget those times
Underrated artists inspired me
To write my life into these lines

I don't know where I'd be without them
But I gotta give all the credit to one more
When I held the blade to my wrist
The Lord told me there's more for my life
So I put down the knife

I write all this down
To inspire hope into your lives
And wont end up in the ground
So take note and don't fantasize about taking your lives

Now to end this off right
I had to get this off my chest
Or I'll never sleep well at night
But for now I think I'll rest

I added Austin's poem because we know this topic is heavy and difficult. Yet he brings a remarkable human touch to serious struggles anyone might encounter and so many of us can relate to. The Value Message here is astounding: *Hope is knocking at your door, it's definitely within reach.*

What just happened?

Something happened to me I can't explain, but it happened. I don't think I've ever been more stressed in my life than when I bought *Big Yellow*, that magical old Victorian era house! Terminating my life had shown itself as an option on much less stressful occasions. Yet this time this option was nowhere to be found.

For whatever reason the *take your life option* for dealing with stress had been removed from the list. I've never struggled with this since. Was I afraid of leaving my family with such a mess? Had all the motivational and personal development propaganda taken root? Was frantically trying to keep my *head above water* distracting me so much that I didn't have time to feel sorry for myself? I recall being so weary with my avoidance tendencies that I was determined to face this challenge head on, no matter what. There certainly was no one else to blame and nowhere to hide. Maybe I was getting a glimpse of my value and worth?

I still can't put my finger on what made such a glaring difference. Something was different from that day forward. I'd be glad for anyone's feedback on this.

No matter who you are I want you to know, *you are far too*

valuable and of too much worth to be thinking them thoughts. Someone told me those exact words more than a decade ago. These words have been a steady light to me. A seed may take a long time to sprout, so don't be discouraged about speaking a Value Message. Planting a timely seed is a beautiful thing.

Chapter 14. Learn baby, learn.

Judge with the mind, not the eye.

Natural eyesight is a gift. Think about how the eyes coordinate with the hands so gracefully. Healthy human eyes can see about one million different colors, have peripheral vision and are capable of discerning great detail. On a clear night, for example, the eye can detect a match being lit on a mountain side, miles away. We become so dependent on keen vision, yet this has some drawbacks.

What we see with the eye contributes to our skewed logic of how we evaluate value. In other words what we see isn't always accurate. We are enchanted by beauty, strength, order and a host of other tangible objects we lay eyes on. Our eyes tire of seeing weakness, chaos, ugliness, poverty and other displeasing sightings. Thus, everything we see is labeled and filtered by what we think is truthful data flowing in front of us. Be cautious when judging with the eye.

(Eccl 1:8 KJV) "The eye is not satisfied with seeing."

The eyes can just exhaust the brain, we need a break. You know how restful it is to close your eyes and disconnect the brain sometimes? Do this often.

If we were blind, we'd all be more spiritual, less judgmental, more curious, listen better and be far clearer on people's *Value Box*! This weariness of what we see, eventually helps us to seek for what we can't see with the eye. Helps us seek beyond our own *nearsightedness*.

Natural resources.

Natural resources, like gas, coal, water, wind and sun are so vital to infrastructure and the economy. No wonder this topic appears in the news and environmental space every day. We couldn't do without these resources, and most are in limited supply. A recent price surge for utilities has been a *pain point* for many of us. Now war breaks out between Russia and Ukraine. Gas prices are offensive. There's no shortage of natural resource shortages.

Do you notice your path intersects with the right people at the right time, on a regular basis? I consider these people a *natural resource*. Perhaps a limited supply, yes, but vital. It will serve you well to be aware of one of the most valuable resources available to you. Often overlooked but right under your nose, other human beings. Be interested, not interesting and you will find more knowledge and wisdom than you can handle.

Haven't you found this to be true? Every person you know has a little or a lot to teach you. Your family, neighbors, friends and strangers. Look around you, it's as if everyone is a messenger with a *Post It note*. Ready to hand you a personal message for your file. People I work with are a bonus, they help me smile every day. I work at a medical facility, from the doctors to the housekeepers, everyone is a resource and always so helpful. When it comes to family resources, I've been fortunate to have won the lottery. Parents, aunts, uncles, cousins, all have been an incredible resource of support and great memories. Even my in-laws have always been in my corner!

For example, our family took a train to Chicago for vacation. Went to the *Cadillac Palace Theater* for a Broadway presentation of *Frozen*. I love all the fancy architecture and city lights. The girls loved the show. My wife loved the coffee. We spent money like confetti, just threw it everywhere. I was bemoaning the money part to the guys I work with, who have kids of their own. Without hesitation they said, "You can always make more money, but you can't always make more memories"! Wow, what a shot to the heart strings.

I'll not soon forget such an indelible Value Message. The message was free, came from a valuable *natural resource* and helped me align my family priorities.

The Doctor is in. What Rachel taught me.

In Elementary School I was not told but shown a lesson about compassion. I've never forgotten this event, but it was a long time before the light came on.

Sheridan Elementary School, Bloomington, Illinois, early 1980's. There was a new girl in school, her name was Rachel. Her family had less than we did, she never had new clothes and often they were not clean. She had no friends and ashamedly kids made fun of her. Despite all this, she was a happy kid. While relieved that kids made fun of her instead of me, I didn't enter into this teasing. Not because I was such a good little boy, certainly I was not. I was afraid dad would find out and I'd be *toast.*

Dad didn't tolerate us making fun of people for something they couldn't help. *Not tolerate,* is putting it lightly. He had Polio as a child and this left him with a deformed leg, perhaps he was the brunt of teasing or bullying, I'm not sure. The thing I was sure of is that serious wrath would be unleashed, had he discovered I was making fun of this little girl. Dad's unyielding view on this subject has been a gift for me that *keeps on giving.* Thanks Dad!

That same year our school got a new principal, Dr. Garrett. What? A Doctor? This was confusing for us fifth graders. After all, the school nurse seemed to be doing a great job. What were those *school people* thinking? We all met Dr. Garrett, who seemed normal enough, he didn't even wear a white coat. He liked us and we all liked him but having a doctor in school seemed *over the top.*

One day in the cafeteria Rachel collapsed on the floor, out like a light! Whoa, us kids had no idea what to do. We couldn't help her because we were afraid to touch her. Here's a metaphor to write home about: You will never help people who you are afraid to touch (and connect with), never ever!

The cafeteria ladies rushed over to her, someone said "Go get Dr. Garrett". Of course, now was for sure an appropriate time to have a doctor *in the house.* Apparently, the adults were thinking ahead for once!

I can still see Dr. Garrett rushing into the cafeteria. He knelt down over Rachel, scooped her up in his arms just like she was his own little girl. Read that again. We could see right away that Dr. Garrett couldn't possibly have cared less about her clothes, her family's economical/social status or if she had any friends. Didn't care about any of that, not at all! And how awesome that he didn't even care in the least bit what all the *gawkers and talkers* were thinking (us kids)! He took her to the nurse's office, called an ambulance and off she went to see yet another doctor. I never did know what happened to Rachel, she was soon back in school, and this never happened again. Maybe she was distraught and collapsed because we didn't know how to befriend her! Shame on us for not seeing her value and not having the courage or skill set to be her friend.

So, for the longest time I thought the *cafeteria incident* was the big part of this story. Guess what... it's not. The bigger part, I promise you, is that Dr. Garrett cared about Rachel on the first day she came to school. He cared about her long before he so carefully picked her up off the floor. The cafeteria was just a place to shine a bright light on the care and compassion he felt toward her already. You will remember teachers who cared about you more than those who educated you.

Dr. Garrett understood Rachel's value before she even came to our school. The Value Message here is: *I care about what I think about you, my friend. Not what others think about you. You are amazing!*

I don't recall one single word Dr. Garrett ever spoke, but I've never forgotten what he did.

Many years have passed since my Elementary School days, but I often remember the lesson. It's no secret, right now our little community has some of the best teachers on the North American continent! The staff here both educate and care about our students. Take time out of your busy day to thank champion teachers in your school district.

"Mr. Gorbachev tear down this wall." -*Ronald Reagan*

This was spoken by Ronald Reagan when there was so much unrest in East Berlin, Germany. I remember the time the Berlin Wall came down, a message heard around the world. Walls may keep others out, but they also keep us in. Berlin proved this all too well. There was mystery about what was on the other side of the wall, no matter which side you were on.

People are on our side more than we think. The opportunity to let us know just doesn't happen often enough. Like Dr. Garrett did with Rachel in the cafeteria. He cared about her, but nobody was aware of this until she collapsed on the floor. Try not to be overly defensive about people, you can let the wall down a bit. You might be surprised at how much people care but don't have the *incident* to show it. Don't wait for a *cafeteria incident* to show people you care about them.

As a parent I am becoming aware of this. I love my kids, but the opportunities to show this in a real way doesn't happen every day. Or does it? At times I'm clumsy at demonstrating this. At times I lose my cool, don't show up as my best self and have to make amends. I look for the occasion to give the message of a hug, randomly and often. When in doubt, err on the side of hugging!

A few years ago, my oldest little girl was obstinate, and I gave her a swat on the leg. Yeah, this was one of my stellar parenting moments. She was upset, crying and said, "Daddy, do you still love me"? Not in a manipulative way, but truly alarmed about being loved. Children being the gifted teachers they are, I learned something never to be forgotten as long as I live. Those words hit me so hard, it broke three of my ribs and cracked a tooth! In my mind I wanted to say, "Of course I do, don't be absurd". I realized how weak and confusing words are to children. They are not in tune with what we say, but what we do and how we act. I knew from that day forward, if my children never heard me speak another word, the message they need to hear from me is "I love you". This must be spoken loud and clear and don't bother opening your mouth to convey it!

Chapter 15. Open your eyes.

"I see," said the blind man to his deaf wife. As he picked up his hammer and saw!

It's difficult to see our own value as we are quite blind to it. Yet easy to perceive value in other people. I find this truth a reality every time a conversation pops up about value. Our perception of people is mostly external. What I mean is, we visually see everyone from their exterior. Their behavior, their actions, apparel, house, car and anything else we see with the eye. Then we pass judgment on all this according to our filters or thinking. As we get to know individuals on a personal level this might change. Our parents, siblings, neighbors and friends just to name a few.

As we interact with people, we begin to understand their inner world of feelings, struggles and emotions. However, the default setting is usually to judge first, ask questions later! Shallow though this might be, we become conditioned to this and think other people do the same thing to us. Which, guess what? They most certainly do!

Seeing the value of other people is so clear and easy. Why are we blind to this virtue when looking within? Are we blind for a reason? Is our blindness the vehicle for our drive to seek and dive deeper into the truth and question of our value? Is the search for our own value a closely guarded secret or simply an extra sense? An extra sense that constantly sniffs out real and genuine truth about our worth. Perhaps a *Judas* lives in all of us, sabotaging this search, according to how willing we are to find it. Suppose we woke up tomorrow and we could see the truth of our own immense value. The first thing that would happen is our *Judas* shows up with a screwdriver and starts trying to poke holes in this truth. It's as if something in us doesn't want to hear or believe a message about our value.

Look through the Johari Window!

Blindness can be explained. How we can be so blind about our behavior yet so clear on the behavior of everyone else. The Johari Window clarifies this. Have you ever heard of this tool? The Johari window is about behavior we are blind to, not value. However, there may be some similarities and besides I've always wanted to promote the Johari Window.

The Johari window is a **technique designed to help people better understand their relationship with themselves and others**. It was created by psychologists Joseph Luft (1916–2014) and Harrington Ingham (1916–1995) in 1955 and is used primarily in self-help groups and corporate settings as a *heuristic* exercise. (Wikipedia)

Heuristic? What's that mean? It means enabling someone to discover or learn something for themselves. Don't try that word out on just anyone, you might get your mouth smacked!

You should take some time to search for this tool on the web. It will save me from trying to explain the details. Group presentations about the Johari windows is one of my favorite activities. It's fun, informative and takes less than an hour.

Here's just a quickie in case your internet is down. Four quadrants, like a small spreadsheet, make up the illustration. Each column and row are labeled, and each quadrant is labeled. The magnitude and power of this tool cannot be overstated IMHO.

Johari Window

	Known to Self	Not Known to Self
Known to others	Open Area	Blind Spot
Not Known To others	Hidden Area	Unknown

1. Open area: Known to others/ known to self (upper left)
2. Blind area: Known to others/ not known to self (upper right)
3. Hidden area: Not known to others/ known to self (lower left)
4. Unknown area: Not known to others/ not known to self (lower right)

Open area: what others know about you, and you know about you. An example might be that you love Chai Tea Latte's. You know it and others know it, but you're the one who gets the *warm fuzzy feeling!*

Blind area: This is the *Big Kahuna*. Wow, can we learn a disgusting amount about other people and especially myself in this quadrant! Tread carefully here, this is where all the arguments on the entire planet start and don't stop! All of us have a blind spot that we cannot see. Others, however, can see with absolute and amazing clarity. Oh, you say, "I'm quite self-aware and surely could discover and see my blind spots". Wrong again sailor! Sure, self-awareness can reduce this quadrant, but there will always be some blindness about us that we just can't see. Yes, regardless of how diligent, honest and self-aware we truly are. Have no fear, no need to be angry, afraid, or embarrassed. Everyone else is the same. No exceptions!

Hidden area: If you can't keep a secret this area will be small. This quadrant is straightforward. An example might be the tattoo on your lower back. *Not known to others,* will differ according to how close the person is to you. Your neighbor might not know about the tattoo, but your spouse will or should! You can create your own list of examples just to get familiar with the window.

Unknown area: This quadrant is also easy to grasp. Think of what would fit here. Maybe you have three kidneys. Unless you have a CT scan, you nor your neighbor would know this about you. Even your spouse would be in the dark about the kidney. Something about myself I learned was I'm afraid of success. Likely this wasn't known about me by me or others. Now this previously *unknown* fact moves to the Open area or Hidden area. The Johari Window is a fascinating tool, I hope you would agree.

Chapter 16. Charity, how great Thou art.

Love is here to stay.

And now abide faith, hope and charity, these three: but the greatest of these is charity. (I Corinthians 13:13 KJV).

Faith and hope are two definite *superpowers,* but both will be obsolete at some point in time. Charity (Love) will never diminish or have a stopping point. Have you ever listened to a song or read a story and was saddened when it ended. Of course, you have, fantasizing what it would be like if it went on forever. Or you've watched a movie over and over, the ending was always the same and you couldn't wait to see it again. The story line connected with us so well or it inspires us emotionally. In any case we just can't get enough of the message.

The story of love is like this, we feel like it's so big and beyond us. I think something within us can sense that love isn't bound by time. Love has an eternal look and feel and beckons us to its euphoric warmth. A good place for the word *Ethereal*!

Incidentally, I have been drawn to a particular song for the past month or so. You know, one I can listen to over and over and I'm sad when it ends. I'm just mesmerized by it, entering into the mind and spirit of the song writer.

U2, *I still haven't found what I'm looking for. The Joshua Tree.* Island Records. 1987.

In case you are wondering. A button on the steering wheel

selects the track. I've listened to the same song for an hour or more while I'm driving. I haven't gotten tired of it yet. Oh, sure, I will sometime but please tell me I'm not the only one who does this!

The Value Message spoken by Love is insanely powerful. Love says, "I will gladly give my life for you". Love says, "You are not a burden". Love is humble, it is kind. It's a pleasure to both give and receive. Love is like a song you never tire of listening to.

The Dance of Romance.

No book would be complete without a romantic scene, so here's my offering. Many love stories are sweet and endearing, but ours is my favorite.

I've told the story about my wife having an accident and this kindled our relationship, though we were acquainted for a long time before this.

She was driving across a bridge when unfortunately, her car went over the side. Fortunately, the front wheel snagged some power lines that were attached on the bridge's edge and dangled precariously above the water. Unfortunately, she was ejected from the vehicle. Fortunately, her leg got tangled in the seat belt and she was now hanging outside the car. Unfortunately, the power lines were sparking, and gas was leaking. Lucky for her I was under the bridge in my houseboat, close by. I motored over so I could reach her and told her I'd rescue her if she would marry me! She reluctantly agreed. Now, looking back, she claims I pressured her into the decision. *Preposterous and accusational,* I say! "The decision is yours, and take all the time you need", I remember emphatically telling her. It was the gentlemanly thing to do. Yet given her two choices, me or the cold, dangerous murky river, she's still wondering if it was the right decision. Hopefully, this experience helped her to have more discernment and be a much better driver.

Well, that's not all true. It was a jon boat. I never did own a houseboat. Okay, honestly, I was the one who fell in love and lucky for me, she signed on the dotted line. Truth be told, my wife says that active listening would be more proof of love than a river rescue.

Adam and Eve.

Mark Twain wrote a humorous story titled: *Extracts from Adam's Diary.*

Twain, Mark, 1835-1910. *The Diaries of Adam & Eve.* Hyattsville, Maryland. Rebecca Press, 1990.

It's written as if the first man Adam kept a diary of those first days, the introduction of the woman and details of how creation started. Adam can't figure out this strange creature who won't leave him alone. Quite the challenge for both. Neither understood the other's behaviors and choices. Both are annoyed and frustrated at times. The humor lies in the accurate description of difficulties men and women face getting to know and relate to each other. Adam and Eve fail to see value in each other, and it shows.

Oh, but let me tell you about two fabulous statements Adam admits to in the end. I think much of Twain's short story mirrors his own life.

At the end, after Eve's passing, Adam says something to this effect: "It would be better to be outside the garden of Eden with Eve, than inside the garden without her". Aww, isn't that so sweet? Reflecting on his growing love for her and realization of her contribution and value.

The other line is a *tearjerker*, I think. Adam concludes: "Wherever Eve was, there was Eden". I take this to mean, she brought life and sparkle wherever she was. I would elaborate a bit further. Maybe Adam was wishing to not have stumbled at the *Ego Box. I should have appreciated the Value Box while the opportunity was there.* He likely was thinking.

Carl and Sally.

Years ago, I met a couple, Carl and Sally. Their children were in their teen years. The boys had gotten in some trouble. I've forgotten now what it was, besides it wasn't the point. Sally was telling the story. As a family this *hiccup* was new territory, mom and dad weren't sure how to handle the situation. This couple had a solid relationship to start with. As the saga unfolded Sally wasn't sure of the outcome of what the right thing to do would even be, nor was Carl. It was left up to Carl to start the conversation with the boys and he did.

Sally was a good storyteller. The emotional stakes were high and it showed. Carl exhibited love, grace and courage with all involved. The situation was soon laid to rest, any wrongs were made right, and everyone gained some wisdom. I knew Sally and Carl were in love to start with. Yet it was touching to hear Sally say, "I fell in love with him again", when she learned even more about the tender heart Carl had toward her children.

Even though some of the details have escaped me, I haven't forgotten the Value Message here. These parents kept a clear vision of their children's value and *Value Box* when it might have been easy to get focused on the mischievous *Ego Box*.

News came a few weeks ago about Carl's sudden passing. What a heart break. He was well respected in the community. His life was a gift to all that knew him. More than six-hundred people attended his funeral, besides friends and family. I would say Carl understood the value of the Value Box of his friends and neighbors and it showed.

Chapter 17. Healing of the nations.

What's up Slumdog?

Boyle, D., & Tandan, L. (2008). *Slumdog Millionaire.* Fox Searchlight Pictures.

Have you watched this movie? In 2009 the movie won eight out of ten Academy Awards it was nominated for. As scenes unfold, so do many *Value Lessons*. The main character, Jamal Malik is answering trivia questions and getting them correct, much to the disappointment of the game show host. Jamal gets the answers right, not because he is so smart, but because of his life experience.

One such experience, even though disgusting, was a winner. The scene flashes back to when Jamal was five years old. After falling into a cesspit, he climbs out to obtain the autograph of a Bollywood star, *Amitabh Bachchan*. He gets the autograph. Everyone in line steps aside, repelled by the awful cesspit stench. Amitabh autographs a paper seemingly not even noticing such foul odor. The Value Message here: *I see your value under all that Sxxt.*

After researching the real Amitabh, I believe this scene accurately portrays his real-life character. In India Amitabh was a National Hero, he connected and empathized with common people. No wonder he was such a hero. When you see people's value, they take notice.

"People will forget what you said, people will forget what you did, but people will never forget how you made them feel." -*Maya Angelou*

Don't be that mean kid.

Tripping a girl at school was one way I played this part. I don't pretend to have been mean only one time either. Being mean can be an addictive habit and quite entertaining when we are bored. The ecstatic feeling, we get from the abuse of power must be similar to the high of crack cocaine. When I was in Junior High School (Bloomington IL) there was this girl who was a good student, had lots of friends and had great rapport with her teachers. I didn't know her personally, didn't even know her name. I had good rapport with my teachers but didn't have a lot of friends and was only a fair student at best.

One day she ran by me in the hall, and I just stuck my foot out, tripping her and spilling her books and paper several feet down the hall. She looked back at me in unbelief. Why would I do this? Why? Mrs. Pritchert came along to investigate what happened as this girl was picking up her *pile*, still staring at me in the same disbelief. She explained to the teacher about how I tripped her. Mrs. Pritchert knew I was a good quiet student and couldn't believe it to be so.

Did I fess up and admit my idiot behavior? Of course not. I just stammered around emphatically denying my involvement and went on to my next class. Mrs. Pritchert never did know or believe I acted out of jealousy and envy. The girl was always so happy and having great fun. She was truly an amazing person no doubt and still to this day is likely wondering what and why about the hall incident. She was having so much fun. I just felt compelled to make her feel bad as a way of making me feel better. By choosing a hurtful act, I exercised the need for power and control.

Where do we learn this stuff? In our nature? We are all capable in regard to being mean. Little boys especially, at about one year old, love to throw rocks. I mean just put a kid next to a pile of small gravel and prove me wrong! So just by nature many of us are stone throwers! It seems we are wired to be mean first and question later, just saying. If you grew up watching much TV, you had a great teacher. How to create cliques and constantly trash talk each other 101! Sitcoms and sarcasm are happily married and have such a charming relationship! Most of this genre will keep you in stitches, I mean what a comic relief to see someone made fun of other than ourselves. It takes a long time to unlearn this mindset.

"Blowing out someone else's candle, doesn't make yours shine brighter!"

"The Toy Story", story.

Lasseter, J. (1995). *Toy Story*. Buena Vista Pictures.

The story of *The Toy Story*, so many lessons to be learned here. This scene comes from the original movie. As always help came from the most unexpected place. Do you remember the toys who were horribly abused? They were terribly disfigured by the neighbor kid. The not so attractive ones who were put together with spare parts. Woody and his buddies had gotten into the neighbor boy's house. Suspense builds as they are surrounded by these *freak* toys. These damaged toys were truly unsung heroes. They proved to be kindly and gentle, offering help to our main characters when they needed it the most.

You've heard *Hurt people, hurt people,* which is so true. However, it is also true, sometimes people who have been hurt by others can empathize on a deeper level and thoroughly touch others from a place of healing and genuineness. As usual I promise you, help will always come to you from the least expected place. I also promise to remind you of this often. Perhaps this is a *God Truth*. Has this been so for you? God never ever helps people in a normal and expected way, ever.

If abuse or violation has been a part of your story, I am so sorry. I'm sorry for what was taken away from you that can never be returned. I'm sorry you felt dirty, I know you felt ashamed and alone. I can't begin to understand how alone and confused and *left behind* you might have felt. I know most people have secrets they can't wait to tell. You had a secret you could not tell, you had to keep it hidden. This was far too much to bear.

At a workshop for at-risk teens, a young woman angrily blurted out to one of the mentors, "You don't know what it's like to be molested and I am so angry". The mentor looked the girl in the eyes and said for all to hear, "When I was molested, I was angry too". For the mentor, this was the first time she had uttered her pain. For the classroom and this young woman there was a message spoken beyond words. A message of value. A message of empathy. A message of hope and a message of healing.

I will say again, "I'm deeply sorry for your hurtful experience". Do you know you have incredible value? Besides this you have the power to heal not only yourself but others also. All the best doctors and medical science know the power of empathy. Everyone in the whole world could learn at your feet. You have empathy and the capacity to make people feel heard. The Value Message that comes from these two weighty items could heal the nations my friend.

Chapter 18. This is how we *role.*

Role with that!

Let's role play some examples of some random questions and see which box is the right fit. Of course, how and by whom messages are spoken make a huge difference. Although these lines look like some type of coding, they are role plays.

Choose one of these two categories. *Spoken* or *Unspoken* messages. The first item will be who is speaking the message: and then the message. After the message is a question, think about what your answer would be. Then, even better than an *open book* test I have written the answer and explanation.

Category: Unspoken messages

Society: "You have worth if you can produce."
Applies to the *Value Box*. True or False?
Answer- FALSE. Skill sets and what you can produce are in the *Ego Box*.

Friend: "I have a better phone than you, loser."
Applies to *Ego Box*. True or False?
Answer- TRUE. Phone is *Ego Box* stuff. I'm not a loser, I see my *Value Box*.

Self: "I missed my goal, I'm worthless."
Applies to Which box?
Answer- *Ego Box*. Yes, I missed my goal. This doesn't change my *Value Box*.

Abuser: "You are dirty and enslaved."
Applies to the *Value Box*. True or False?
Answer- FALSE. Your *Value Box* is clean and free. Discover this truth.

Culture: "You aren't like me. You must be inferior."
Applies to which box?
Answer- BOTH. Yes, the *Ego Box* is different. No, I'm not inferior, my *Value Box* is the same as yours.

Category: Spoken messages

Person: "You are ugly."
Applies only to *Ego Box*. True or False?
Answer- TRUE. *Value Box* is unaffected and so what? No reflection on the *Value Box*.

Person: "You are beautiful."
Applies only to the *Value Box*. True or False?
Answer- FALSE. Applies to *Ego Box* and so what? No reflection on the *Value Box.*

Person: "You are such a loser."
Applies only to *Ego Box*. True or False?
Answer- TRUE. Even if it's true, this only applies to the *Ego Box.*

Grandma: "You are beautiful."
Applies to the *Value Box*. True or False?
Answer- TRUE. She is speaking to your *Value Box*. Likely not focusing on the *Ego Box.*

Father: Breaks your clarinet, says, "You will never amount to anything".
Which box?
Answer- *Ego Box* only. *Amounting to anything* is irrelevant, simply an opinion.

Abuser: "You are the cause of all our problems."

Which box?

Answer- *Ego Box* only. Even if the statement is true, the *Value Box* is unaffected.

Role play is a widely used and effective communication tool. These role play examples may be kind of rugged but serve the purpose of pointing our mind to think outside the box. This play can help sort out the cacophony of messages we are pelted with every day. Role play offers a safer exploratory environment for us.

I'm thinking about how these examples could be expanded and clarified to be more useful and relevant. Creating Flash Cards for example or inventing a board game with this subject matter. Keep your eye on my website for updates. I'm excited.

The good news.

When I was a child, a particular hymn drew me to its message. *Was it for me,* was the title. One of the captivating lines was, "Was it for me, yes all for me. Oh, love of God so great so free..."

Whyte, John M. *Was it for me?*

I was hearing a message of incredibly good news. Yet was this good news for me? Wasn't it for good people? People who were perfect? I thought of so many reasons and excuses that this message wasn't for me. You know, so many earthly things are simply out of our reach. Like fame and fortune. New clothes. Enough food. Love and belonging. Safety, hope, mercy and the list goes on and on. I wanted it to be true, but I couldn't completely believe it could be possible. Except for other people, anything is possible for other people. The question, "could it be for me", just quietly simmered in the back of my mind for decades.

As the years go by, the shadows of doubt are fading. The love of God is simply beyond the scope of what the human mind can digest.

Can I just say a little more about perceiving our own value? We want to believe we have value. We want it to be true. We are just dying to find even the smallest amount of rock-solid evidence. One minute someone gives us hope, another minute a wave of doubt crashes down on us. Society, culture and our own minds gang up on us. They are like ocean waves, steady and relentless.

Despite all this noise and turmoil, I want to remind you about a message of incredibly good news. Your value and worth is *off the charts*!

Chapter 19. Listen deeply.

Another great story!

"Always leave people better than you found them. Hug the hurt, kiss the broken, befriend the lost and love the lonely." *-Richard Hagen*

True story. Meet again Dr. William Glasser. I highly recommend this author. He has some disruptive things to say about education, society and psychiatry. Dr. Glasser's book *Warning Psychiatry can be hazardous to your mental health,* is a tremendous read.

Glasser, William Dr. *Warning Psychiatry can be hazardous to your mental health.* USA: Harper Collins, 2004.

In Glasser's book, Al Siebert writes of his own experience, forcibly committed to the psych ward. He was studying Psychology and was thinking outside the box, something his educators had clearly instructed him to do. As a psychologist he also shares some stories of patients he worked with. One such story is of a young woman named Molly, who was admitted to the psychiatric ward. This was the era when Thorazine was the *solve the problem drug* of choice. Prescribed to thousands of mental health patients, high on numbing effect, low on results.

Molly's doctors were ready to commit her to the State Hospital Psychiatric Ward because she quit talking to anyone, furthermore she also claimed God had talked to her. Can you believe the audacity! Who wouldn't agree that she needed to be committed? Yes, I'm kidding!

Mr. Siebert asked if he could perform a few psychological tests on Molly before she was transferred. Permission was granted so an appointment was set up. Al had prepared some questions for Molly. Questions like, "What would happen if I just listened to her and don't allow my mind to put any psychiatric labels on her. What would happen if I talked to her believing that she could turn out to be my best friend"?

Questions were what got Al involuntarily committed to the psych ward in the first place. This man was a brilliant mind and found himself in serious trouble after questioning his wife, the Church and the Psychiatric establishment. Al's searching excerpt in Glasser's *eye opening* book should be mandatory reading.

On their first meeting Al asked his prepared questions and a few more. Molly shared that she had sought approval from her parents but found none. As an example, she got first chair playing the clarinet in the high school orchestra. Feeling sure dad would be proud of her for this, he was not. Just to prove it, he broke her clarinet on the table and said she *would never amount to anything.* You know this wasn't an isolated incident. You can be sure Molly was getting a steady barrage of the "you are worthless" message. She had some relationship difficulties in college and a boyfriend ended his relationship with her. Molly found herself in an extreme state of loneliness, gaining her a spot on the Psych Ward.

This story has a profound Value Message that struck a chord with me the first time I read it. I'll talk more about this later. When asked about God speaking to her, Molly said. "I felt like the most special person in the whole world". Visits with Molly were encouraging, and she seemed to be improving.

Do you know what happened next? Yes, I'll bet you do. I wouldn't even have to tell the rest of the story, but I will. The following paragraph is directly from Glasser's book.

At the morning reports during the next week, we heard that Molly was talking to people, participating in ward activities, dressing better, and wearing makeup. The plan to commit her was postponed. The supervising psychiatrist said, "This may be a case of spontaneous remission. You can never predict when it will happen."

Molly's story was pivotal for me. I started to see people through a different lens. Started judging less. Started being more curious and listening more. Started asking more questions and started thinking more outside the *box*. The *Ego Box* especially!

In a later visit Molly asked Dr. Seibert if he thought God actually spoke to her, or did she just imagine this. I can't be one hundred percent sure about the answer to her question.

However, I can tell you my truth about her question. Having children has taught me about God speaking to people. When we are vulnerable, hurt and lonely, we may be the readiest to listen to God and any message he would have for us. God's message is always different from what we are accustomed to in this world, as Molly found out.

If my children were somewhere facing a difficult experience, lost, alone, afraid or on the Psych Ward with limited communication from me or if I were dead, I'd want them to hear and understand this message: "I love you, you have value and furthermore you are the most important person in the world to me!"

Have you ever been distraught about something, and no one seemed to care or listen? Do you know how therapeutic it is just to feel heard? It's much better than medicine. Believe it or not, you are completely worthy of being heard. Being *heard* will be one of the most powerful Value Messages you will ever speak. We all crave to be heard and known. Dr. Seibert's simple and genuine listening when needed most was the Value Message responsible for getting Molly out of the Psych Ward.

The consistent steady verbal vomit of, "You will never amount to anything, you are worthless", was the message that got her into the Psych ward.

The two messages of, "You are worth something" and "you are worth nothing" are at war with one another. Most of us struggle in this conflict every day. This conflict comes from being *on the fence* about value. Wherever you are, you will find warriors with many a battle scar, weary of this tiresome skirmish. Wherever you are, you will find opportunities to take sides. It seems to me that Dr. Siebert understood Molly's real value and gave her space to see the truth about it. I've got some more real good news for you here. Every person on the planet can be involved in this dogfight. Why? Because everyone has what it takes or can learn what it takes to make a difference. Listening, a smile, kindness, curiosity and friendship goes a long, long way baby! Especially listening.

Hearers are plentiful, *listeners* are powerful!

Reflecting on Molly's story, I want to explore more about listening. Everyone has heard admonitions as to the wisdom of listening. If this skill is so important, why is it not offered as a subject in school or college? Don't spend time pondering that question. Instead take time to learn this mighty skill on your own. Listening can be encouraged but difficult to teach.

Am I a good listener? I do consider myself a good listener, but the more I know about listening, the less I know about listening. Listening is true empathy personified. Interestingly listening and empathy aren't the same thing, but it's impossible to cultivate one without growing the other. Is it possible that we are afraid of listening? To listen is to let go. Let go of ideals, traditions, mindsets and comfort zones. Show me a good listener and I'll show you a person with empathy, I'll show you a leader and I'll show you someone who connects with people. *Hearers* are plentiful, *listeners* are powerful.

So powerful is the art of listening that I've dedicated an entire webpage to this subject at thevaluemessage.com/listening. Check out the links on my website for more information. Listening, though a necessary skill is not complex, my web page mostly consists of web links to *Thought Leaders* speaking about the skill of listening. This isn't to say speaking isn't important, it's just that we all know there's a reason we have two ears and only one mouth.

Listening is an *undecorated* hero and skill set. Compared to talking, yelling, persuading and screaming. Listening is *low profile*. It's a vacuum compared to an explosion. Yet listening has altered the tide of war. Has softened hatred. Turned enemies into friends. Saved countless lives and calmed the masses. What other power or skill can boast of such things?

A TEDx talk I highly recommend is given by William Ury. (*The power of listening: William Ury, TEDxSanDiego*). Mr. Ury's entire career has centered around the power of listening. He has worked with National Leaders, high level business executives and countless other groups.

"Seek first to understand then to be understood." -*Steven R. Covey*

Did God say?

Let me add a few words about God speaking to Molly. I hope you don't think this is irreverent or sacrilegious, but along with her doctors, God also was aware of Molly's case. God raised an eyebrow about the messages she was receiving long before she or her doctors were aware of any sign of trouble. "I need someone to send a message to Molly about her value, even if it's just a small one. Surely her parents will do this" God thought. "Oops, I guess that's not going to work. Let's see, maybe her teachers or fellow students will show up with a message of hope. Hmmm, not there either, what about her boyfriend? Could he be the one with the message? I guess not him either."

"Now about the boyfriend", God might further ponder. "Right now, he isn't in the position to see the *Value Box*. Maybe ten years down the road he will see people differently, but not right now." "Let's just give him some time to 'percolate' and see what happens."

God, now getting a little anxious about the situation. Alarmed at the dismal prognoses of the State Psychiatric Ward, decides to take action. God says to himself, "I'll just talk to Molly personally, give her a little spark of hope and see what happens". So, he did just that. "Molly, I want you to know, you are important to me." He whispered.

Now here is what happens with Molly. She gets this feeling, like she is the most important person in the world. "Whoa, what was that? What in this world is going on? It feels like God just told me I was the most important person in the world. I haven't had a feeling or heard anything like that in my entire life. 'OMG!'

Who can I tell about this? Not a soul, they all think I'm seriously crazy anyway. I'm just going to stop talking to everyone, because everything I hear is nothing like what I just heard", she says to herself.

God then sees Dr. Siebert coming into the picture and says, "Whew, Al will have a message about her value, so he can take it from here. I don't need to say anything further to Molly, in time she will have an understanding about her value."

Chapter 20. Take a look inside.

You are unique like the rest of us.

That we are unique is another commonality among us. All incredible lives matter. What do you mean, we are all the same and have more common ground than we'd care to admit? I'm over it and I look for the common traits in my fellow peeps. People crave to be unique and different, but is this just another attempt to feel valued and appreciated? "I'm unique and I'm totally pleading with you to see me for who I am". Is that what's being said? We cut our hair, wear jeans riddled with holes, buy products and get tattoos to portray individualism. Then we hang out with people doing the same exact thing, which now is *groupism*! We have a strong desire to be both unique and blend in with the crowd at the same time.

I look for common ground because I want to belong. Yet we can be the same and unique at the same time! Sometimes we search for differences to reassure ourselves that we are better than someone else, but this is playing with the *Ego Box*. We search for this common ground to feel connected and understood. To see others on the same level, we'll have to let go of labeling and the many levels of the *better than you* mindset.

There's a book for that! Yes, my author friend Dr. William Glasser clarifies this identifying behavior in his book titled: *The Identity Society*.

Glasser, William. *The Identity Society.* USA. Harper & Row, 1972.

If you are a salesperson, this book would especially serve you well. If you are wondering what's up with all the trends and fads, this book is also for you. Dr. Glasser writes in great detail about how and why behavior is dictated by how we identify with people, trends, products and more. Not *you are a good or bad boy* type of behavior. More like what and why we buy products, who we connect with and why we pay good money for a bad pair of jeans! An enlightening book, high on my recommended reading list.

At our high school graduation, for example, we were inspired to know our class was one of the best and brightest. We could grab the future by the horns and sail to new heights on determination and Mountain Dew! Then I learned that the class before and after us was the best and dang smart too. How could this be? This *positive spin* message heard at such events loses its charm after a more realistic version of life emerges. Although we do need an extra boost to leave the nest, most parents are doing everything they can to encourage the next steps in life for the kids. Here again, it's possible for everyone to be unique. Appreciating the other person's attributes and skills can help us and we don't have to be any less unique or valuable.

A Rodeo friend of mine gave me an insight into this identity phenomenon. Like many sports or trades, it's all about the clothing. Cowboys identify strongly with a particular brand of clothing. You don't even think of wearing any other brand at the Rodeo and shirk the idea of having anything else in your own home. Yes, the hat is important too. You keep the $400 special hat in a tight box just for race day, nothing else. Brands of other persuasions have tried unsuccessfully for years to squeeze into the market. My advice to marketers: Try to find a less stubborn unique group.

You are Special.

Mr. Fred Rogers wrote a book titled: You are Special

Rogers, Fred. *You are special*. USA: Penguin, 1995.

Great book. I didn't get into Mr. Rogers as a youth, but as an adult his message resonates with me. I appreciate the message and language he spoke to millions of children. For years his show aired on public television. "You are unique", I can hear him saying this often. "There's no one else in the world like you", he would impress on his audience. The message he was clearly trying to convey was about your innate value. Even though our uniqueness is in the *Ego Box*.

I will always believe Mr. Rogers's pointed message was intentional, empowering and refreshingly counterculture. Thanks for your vote, Fred!

You are enough, self-love and self-care.

You read and hear about these topics more than ever. How would you define selfishness? I have misused this label (selfish) for far too long. My definition of selfishness has changed considerably with time and observation. The picture in my mind simply needed to change as the old picture wasn't serving me well at all, nor was it accurate.

There was a time when the picture in my mind of selfishness looked something like this: A person who thought of their own self instead of others. Someone not engaged in physical labor. Someone not fitting into accepted norms or who would question authority. Someone with the luxury of leisure time, laying out at the beach, enjoying life while others could not. As you can see, this is my own perspective. The perspective I knew to be coming from a place of correct judgment and stuff! (Laughing hysterically)

Selflessness had a different definition. Hard work, unquestioning *the plan,* taking one for the team no matter how it affected you. Spending yourself to please everyone else without thought of any social or spiritual expense to you. Anyone who didn't conform to my definition was sure to be labeled and shamed, if not by words, for sure in my mind.

You are totally enough. Repeat after me, "I am enough". Look in the mirror, look yourself in the eye and say, "You are enough". Seriously, repeat these words at least ten times. Do this in the morning and at night until you feel no objections from within. Be patient, give yourself the time it takes. This would be a great time and place for the affirmations we talked about earlier.

Let's talk coffee shops.

The aroma and message coming from your local coffee shop is quite the study. The message patrons hear in these places of greatness has *self-care* written all over it.

Fancy coffee is probably second only to the spa industry for prodigal spending. That people consider a massage or facial a self-indulgence is no argument. Manicures and Pedi's too. Oh, what a feeling and no one cares too much about the price. Honestly, I'm still a little shy about the personal touch that goes with a massage or facial. I'm going to take a cue from my friend Norrell and call for an appointment soon though.

Do you remember when this coffee culture came to your town? Betcha heard a lot of people scoffing at that four-dollar cup of coffee. Betcha those same people were wishing they had bought stock in one of those big chains. Betcha if they started charging twenty dollars a cup people would find a way to afford it! Why? Because extravagant hot coffee is a wonderful message! What a great way to tell ourselves and others, "I'm totally taking care of myself and it feels awesome, no apologies". If there's a crowd, we get the benefit of feeling noticed, a sense of belonging, which also delivers that beloved shot of dopamine. To top this off, the probability of a bar fight breaking out is almost non-existent.

We have a unique coffee shop in our small town (don't they all). *The Local Brew.* Find us on Facebook! Rushville IL. A real success. I am so surprised at the customer base. People I would never suspect show up and get their *fix,* happy as clams. I want to belong, so I sanction every Friday afternoon for a visit. Spiced Chai, two shots of vanilla, large, hot! The retail space for this venue is less than 150 square feet. Yet purveyors of happiness and belonging they are, and it shows! My wife buys the *merch.* You know, that term my kids taught me. Short for *merchandise,* these are the shirts, hoodies and insulated cups you can also purchase to heighten the sense of belonging! People are thirsty for much more than coffee. Thirsty for a group hug, basically. The Value Message here is: *We appreciate you and you should appreciate you!* "If you feel the same, leave a tip."

You are enough.

What does this mean? I personally love this, because it is a strong message and artillery barrage against the cultural message that echoes: "You *are* not enough! You *are* not enough. You will *never* be enough. Why would you ever think you *are* enough? No matter how hard you try, you will not be enough." Sound familiar? It should, this message is so loud and caustic, how could it be missed. "You *are* not enough" is an Ego message. "You *are* not enough" is a selfish, loathing message laced with shame. "You *are* not enough" is strongly bound to my own expectation of you. "You *are* not enough" is a message completely void of the capacity to see your value in any way. "You *are* not enough" is a message without hope. Why? Because it speaks to your lack and reeks of a scarcity mindset.

You are not enough is a cancerous message and beckons you to spend and search until you arrive at *enough*. Guess what? Culture and society will never be satisfied with your *enough*. They will never be satisfied with your *Ego Box*. It does not matter how much or what you do, you will never be enough. You get straight A's. You are super smart. You get first chair in the High School Orchestra. You are beautiful. You are skinny. You are strong and mighty. You are a Kung Fu master. You speak three languages. You are whatever else. "Sorry, Charley", but when your abilities have entertained us, we are moving on to the next thing. The Value Message here is like a needle in a haystack... don't even bother looking, it's not there.

You are enough is like a cup of cool water, but sometimes we don't know why. This just sounds so good and refreshing and trendy, so I believe it, I want to believe it. Yet I'm still not sure what it means or why I should like it. Right now, I just noticed I've repeated *You are enough* about one hundred times in my head. As if this repetition will clarify the definition for me. The *you are enough* message speaks of the *Abundance* mindset. No other *props* are needed. Yet *you are enough* is scary, it's so counterculture. *You are enough* is not about conceit or arrogance, nor pride. On the contrary I find it to be about humility and grace. If I can be nice to me, I can be nice to you. *You are enough* is not implying that you have *arrived*, or no improvement is needed. *You are enough* isn't hampering personal growth or potential. It's giving you space and energy to expand your *footprint*.

Humility and grace? What else? *You are enough* is freedom. Freedom from the *Ego Box* and its struggle to be the best and most. Freedom from the *volatility* of our value and self-worth rising and falling like the stock market. Freedom from the insecurity of losing our position, possessions or abilities. *You are enough* says, "I see my own value and I have nothing to prove". Could it actually be that simple?

Society doesn't speak the "You are enough" message so loudly. Maybe it's our consumerism culture. We are conditioned to think we can hardly survive without some product we must have because everyone else has. Or you can't be enough unless you are attached to someone or something. *You are enough* is a mindset, not an amount!

Props and crutches.

Even the tough independent type must have their products. Beer, jeans, knives or that brand of car or clothing. We send a message by the products we choose. Nothing wrong with this. It's just difficult to survive without our *prop* or *crutch* to hold us up or give us courage. Most of us can't stand on our own two feet without a shot of courage. We need that brand name shoe, or we can barely walk.

Clothes are the same way. I get insecure if I go out of the house without my favorite brand of boxers on. I'm insecure about running around the yard in my birthday suit. That's a joke by the way! Do you see what I mean though? *You are enough,* all by itself, without *props* or *crutches*, is unfamiliar to us.

Unless we see at least a little bit of our own value and *Value Box*, it will be difficult to comprehend what is meant by, *you are enough*. How would you define, *you are enough*? I'm curious. Write down your answer, post it on the bathroom mirror or somewhere you will see it often. These three words (you are enough) come to mind when a baby is born naked into this world. Do we look for a newborn child to bring us some gift or talent? How big is their *Ego Box*? Isn't he or she the gift? Isn't the child enough already? The Value Message here is: *I see you for who you are, and you are enough.*

The Greatest Showman and Show Woman.

You are enough is a message well portrayed in the movie, *The Greatest Showman.* Let me tell my side of the story.

Gracey, M. (2017). *The Greatest Showman.* Twentieth Century Fox.

Our whole family loves this movie. Drama. Romance. Music. Royalty. Power struggles. Fire. What's not to love about this show? My wife of course doesn't like watching movies with me as you can imagine. I'm an emotional roller coaster.

The man who eventually became P.T. Barnum's father in-law treated the young P.T like dirt, smacking him in the face in the presence of his father. Quite the Value Message, he never forgot it. As you know Barnum had an insane amount of drive and ambition. Much of this, if not all, was to convince his father in-law Mr. Hallett, that he indeed had value and worth. Tragically this story is all too common. Hallett not only couldn't see Barnum's *Value Box*, but he would also refuse to see it if it was handed to him on a silver platter. Sadly, because of stubbornness and pride I suspect he would choose death over revealing any hint of admiration or value to such a scoundrel and showman as he knew his son in-law, Barnum to be.

Side Note: There was a clear separation of classes in the movie. For example, the way Mr. Hallett treated the young P.T. and his father, and they tolerated this! Intimidated by power and social status. My advice for this day and age... DO NOT try slapping a child in the presence of his father. Power nor status will protect you from the wrath to come. You will find yourself racking up some hefty medical expenses or possibly need the services of an undertaker.

What a powerful character Charity played, Barnum's wife. She was all about the *Value Box.* Not at all enchanted with the *Ego Box,* she was able to shine when they had few worldly goods, clearly, she could see everyone's *Value Box.* She longed for her husband to see this also, but at the time he could not. Charity was most contented and at rest knowing how valuable their children were, and the togetherness of a family. She could see Barnum's *Value Box* and it mattered not at all that her own parents refused to see this. Such is the story of love.

Ironically, it was Barnum who instilled a sense of value and self-worth in the hearts and minds of his curious circus crew. These talented characters, though *social misfits*, were quite amazing with their gifts. The Greatest Showman inspired them to rise far above the hurtful sneer of the crowd. This gave them the needed space and time to see their own true value. In the end they would approve of themselves, regardless of how the crowd judged them. The crowd did eventually love them and hopefully learned a lesson about how to treat and appreciate people for who they are. The inspiring message I hear from this circus troupe is the message I will repeat more than once in this book. *If others see your value, you are advantaged. If you see your own value, you are unshakable*!

Now at the end of the movie, the *happy ending* is unfolding for us! Barnum sells his part of the business and sees the *Ego Box* for what it is and now doesn't need to prove anything to anyone. He gets a better picture of his own value and certainly that of his children and wife. Perhaps simply a result of being disillusioned with the *Ego Box*. What a glorious ride to the theater on that massive elephant where the girls are performing. Running up the stairs signaling that he is fleeing and gladly leaving what is behind him. The camera pans in on the couple seated in the theater watching the show, enjoying each other's company truly united in heart and mind.

Charity was a picture of strength, grace and beauty throughout the show. But do you remember how she broke out in an incredible smile, sort of cozying up to Barnum in the theater seat as they watched the ballet recital? That smile was brighter than the noon day sun. I don't know how the producers made that happen, but they did. This was a case of a picture being worth a thousand words. Obviously, you know my bias here about value, but I think she was exceedingly happy that Barnum could see the reality and truth of the *Value Box*. His own, hers and theirs.

The Value Message here: *Your value does not decrease because of someone's inability to see your worth.*

Self-love.

"Maybe it's not too late to learn how to love and forget how to hate." *Ozzy Osbourne*

It will be difficult to love others until we love ourselves. It's like we have to learn the ropes by getting a feel for how this works on us. It's the discovery and practice of the Golden Rule! Loving oneself and seeing our own value is close to the same thing.

Self-love gets a bad rap, so let's look at it closely. Why the bad rap? Labels of course. Self-love sounds so different from the *hero trait* of being selfless. Selflessness has a martyr quality. It is a virtue unless an ulterior motive is involved. The ulterior motive could be to generally manipulate someone for personal gain. We tend to label self-love as scary and alarming or narcissistic. After anything is labeled, we tuck it away somewhere snuggly and forget about it, having no desire or reason to explore this any further. Unfortunately, we tend to do this with everything we label, people especially.

When I dug deeper into what self-love could mean, my interest grew. It's like the *snowball effect*. The more we love ourselves, the more we will value ourselves. The more we value ourselves, the more we value others. The easier it will be to see our *Value Box.* The better we will take care of ourselves. The less apt we will be to destroy ourselves. The less power, addictions will have over us. The more we'll think about how others see themselves. Self-love and selfishness are completely different animals. Be clear on this.

Self-care.

Remember my friend Norrell? I hadn't heard from him for a long time. One day he sent me a picture on Facebook, a close up shot of his face. I didn't know if he'd been hit by a car or had passed out. Apparently, he was having a facial done. He told me it was the most relaxing thing he ever did! He was helping a friend manage some spas and must have been testing out the product!

I started reading some of his Facebook posts. He spoke a lot about self-care and its wisdom. Years ago, I thought I'd create and market *relaxation CDs*, try to help people fall asleep at home, not in the car. Sharing this with Norrell he said, "people won't relax unless you tell them to". I'm finding that to be so true. People won't take action or do activities because someone hasn't given them permission to do so. You may need this kind of permission for relaxation and self-care. If this is you, I now give you permission to practice self-care and relax. I feel like a doctor who just whipped up a prescription for his worried patient. You can pay me later!

Why does this formality of getting permission from yourself or others show up? I'm curious about this. Let's just use self-care as an example. Are we afraid of disapproval? Are we uncomfortable with this idea and at least need to self-talk our way into this? It's not like we are robbing a bank ya know. Do we need the *alter-ego* of our parents in our self-talk to say, "Yes, Son, this is wholesome and good for you, I approve"? Maybe it's because self-care is out of our comfort zone, and we need a little push to cross the line.

Self-care is not to be taken lightly. You will be teaching people how to treat you, beginning with how you treat you. You can only help others with what flows out of your bucket. Meaning our lives must be full of grace, resolve, joy, love, hope, kindness, wisdom and whatever. As these flow out from us (our bucket so to speak), others are helped by the *overflow.* We help others from our abundance, not our scarcity. You must practice what you preach.

Lena Kay at lenakay.com. was asked in an interview, "Who is the most important person in your life right now?" "I am, most definitely I am", she said. To further explain this she says, "you can't take care of others unless you take care of yourself". This seemed profound to me, not long ago I would have thought this to be conceited and selfish. Not at all. What a great truth this is. Self-care isn't always indulgence or doesn't have to be defined as such. Indulgence was the picture that came to mind for a long time when thinking about self-care. Is there virtue in choosing the opposite of self-care? Self-loathing for example? Never setting boundaries, exhausting yourself to meet or exceed the expectation of others? Does burning the candle at both ends help us to grow and learn? Does this set us up for success? Will burning ourselves out enable us to be our best self in service to others? Not to mention how we are teaching others to treat us. Self-care isn't just the Spa treatment, or the gratification of external luxuries. More importantly it's the practice letting go of what disrupts our internal peace. Self-awareness needs to accompany self-care. This would be the *mature* thing to do. Being aware of what you do and how you act while practicing self-care is accountability.

When I was so stressed and freaked out about buying the big yellow house, I practiced self-care. Relaxation didn't show up for quite a while, but self-care did, I guess. I was apt to totally come *unglued* and have an emotional meltdown. At the time, the default setting was to stick my head in the sand and let someone else figure it out. Instead, I woke up early every day consuming motivational speeches, podcasts, affirmations and all things useful in the *self-help* space. This didn't look like the indulgent type of self-care, but I was becoming the most important person in my life! Why because I knew if I didn't grow and take care of myself, there was no way I could take care of anyone else. Namely my family and those who depended on me or counted on me to *make it happen.*

Self-care should involve your physical and mental capacities. Don't just do the spa and fancy coffee on the outside and not show *the love* to the inside. It's great if you can show others how to treat you. Show you how to treat you. I can't emphasize this enough.

For example, show yourself some compassion. Forgive yourself, be kind when you make a mistake. Learn from a misstep. Let your mind know what's good for the outside is good for the inside too. Before you know it, you and your own self will be friends!

I forgive myself for...

I was in line at Walgreens a few years ago, both check-out

lines were backed up. The customer at the other counter didn't have enough money, a few dollars short. The line was long, and tension was growing. She went to the car to search for some spare change, how humiliating. I was paying for my items at the other register. I didn't pass the test. In fact, I got a big fat "F".

I had twenty dollars in my pocket, could have gotten cash back and helped her. The crowd was staring and waiting. So, I just grabbed my unnecessary items and left. I walked past an older car with five kids inside, later realizing this was her dilapidated vehicle.

Many times, I've wondered how different the outcome would have been if I'd turned around and put some cash in her bag while she was searching the floorboards for a few bucks. What if others in line would have taken my que and she could have had a few hundred dollars to help buy some groceries? Or I could have offered to take them all out to eat and spend some time with the kids. It was a long time before I forgave myself for not doing different and better. Being more mindful of the opportunity to help others is the only redeeming factor from that experience. To the lady at Walgreens that day... I'm sorry and thank you for letting me get that *off my chest*.

I've wept in the night for shortness of sight,
That to somebody's need made me blind.
But never as yet felt a tinge of regret,
For being a little too kind.

Chapter 21. Application Mountain.

Next stop? Believe the reality of your value.

Not just because I told you so. You must experience seeing your value and worth from your own eyes. When Hologram pictures were first introduced, I was looking at a book with all these strange images. I tried to follow the helpful instructions everyone was giving me. Crossed my eyes, held the book close to my face and moved it away. Wondering what I was even looking for. Maybe I should just act like I see something and move on, I thought!

Suddenly an image appeared within the picture, in time the eye sort of caught on to the drill and more easily found the hidden picture. All the well-meaning and enthusiastic persuasion of my friends did not make me a believer. It had to be *felt, not telt.* This optical confirmation then put a stop to the gears of my brain trying to figure out what I could not see but was supposed to.

My wife's grandpa was having a difficult time with this technology. He did his best to see these elusive images, in earnest trying to follow every instruction. All of us *believers* are now on the edge of our seats waiting for his revelation to come. It must have been an hour of fruitless effort when grandpa said, "Do you have to have both eyes"? Oops, none of us remembered that Nobert could only see out of one eye. We were all sort of heart broken, because it's not possible to enjoy this art without both eyes working together. Sometimes no amount of explaining or instruction or passion will help the mind see what the eyes understand.

Isn't this another good place for one of my favorite quotes?

You are advantaged if others see your value, you are unshakable if you see your own value!

Apply now.

How to apply what you are aware of? It's too late, your prodigious brain is already on the search for ways to apply this information. For example, right now, don't you feel some movement in the back of your mind? Thinking about some personal interactions you've had and how the *Value Box* and *Ego Box* was involved. Have you ever looked back at past conversations or confrontations and wished they could be redone? absolutely! You are not alone. It's the application of what we learn that helps us successfully *climb the mountain.*

When to apply the brake and when to apply the gas is one of the most important skills when learning to drive a car. Avoiding obstacles and ensuring the safety of your passengers are also priorities. That's so like what you need to do right now. Any mindset changes or personal development effort has an awkward learning stage. Knowing when to apply the brake or gas takes practice, it may mean some close calls or even getting stuck in the ditch. You can ignore the gawkers who drive by with a smug look on their face. Pay attention and show appreciation to the ones who take time to stop and help you get out of the ditch.

Awareness is on your side, when it wakes up, it won't go back to sleep! The truth is your unconscious mind may have figured out the two boxes long ago and is patiently waiting for your conscious mind to catch on.

I find myself applying the *Value Box/Ego Box* filter everywhere. Why we do what we do or don't do. What would have made the difference in each scenario. Why did this person treat someone that way, good or bad? I look at human interactions based on the focus of these two boxes. This means the results are somewhat predictable.

Learn to be an observer, don't let your analytical side work too hard though, otherwise at the end of the day your mind will be exhausted. This would be a great time for some mediation, something restful, some self-care. When it comes to positive self-improvement, *direction* is more important than *speed.*

Celebrate wins no matter how small. Practice this often, when you find yourself being more thankful, celebrate. A little better at setting boundaries? Celebrate. Listening to the other person's point of view more often? Celebrate. Celebrating your wins is another way to foster self-care. No need to even spend money on this option. Celebrating can look like a walk to get fresh air, a glass of ice water or a few Jumping Jacks. Just get in the habit of generating positive energy around celebration.

Moving forward the messages you tell yourself will carry weight. You're more aware of how impactful words and thoughts are. The messages you allow yourself to listen to will need permission to pass through your ears. Some will be accepted, some will not. You are worth every effort on your part. No one else's permission is needed for you to see and appreciate your value. You are incredible. You are enough.

Bonus round.

1. To improve your mood: exercise
2. To think more clearly: meditate
3. To understand the world: read
4. To understand yourself: write
5. To help people: help yourself
6. To learn faster: have fun

Be Thankful!

Be thankful every day, embrace an abundance mindset and do the work! Being thankful is free, anyone can do this. It's also freeing. If you can be more thankful, freedom will follow. You will be much easier to live with! Gratitude has no downside. It helps you and everyone around you.

Every time I open the fridge, I'm thankful. When I was a kid, there were times the fridge had nothing in it. To this day I always have a *peaceful, easy feeling*, when I see food in the refrigerator. Think of this, Solomon in all his glory never even dreamed of such an appliance. He had hundreds of wives and lots of gold, but did he have a refrigerator? No! Cold milk, cold cheese, leftovers, food in jars, in drawers anytime day or night. It's a great day to be alive. Not to mention electricity that enables the refrigerator to work. Oh, and don't get me started on the virtues of running water and indoor plumbing.

An old preacher friend I knew, Dorne Garner, talked about visiting a family in Enid Oklahoma about 100 years ago now. Seven family members in this humble home, Dorne and his coworker made nine, Saturday night was *bath night*. There was one washtub, only filled one time. Dorne was the last to use it. I wonder which body wash and conditioner they used. This weekly bathing routine was the rule, not the exception, I'm sure. Indoor plumbing, what a *Godsend* when it came along. If you are reading this book and don't have indoor plumbing, contact me. I'll get you connected with the right people.

My ice maker is like the cruise of oil and barrel of meal that *failed not* in the Old Testament (1 Kings 17:16 KJV). I take the ice out of the freezer and the next day it's full again. In the summer I dump the ice hopper in a cooler. Next day, it's full again, a modern-day miracle! Just sayin'.

What about when life takes a *nosedive*? When loss or hardship comes about? Thankfulness may not just come pouring out of us, some things we were grateful for may even seem superficial. Yet if we become familiar with thankfulness every day, our mindset will be in sync with the language of gratitude, and we'll be less apt to be derailed when the going gets tough.

Here is a simple *thankfulness exercise* for you.

Write down five things you are thankful for every morning for seven days. No duplicates, each item must be different. At the end of the week, you will notice a difference.
A gratitude journal is another *eye opener*. Reserve a page to write down what you are thankful for. Go to this often and reflect.

If at first finding something to be thankful for is difficult, don't be discouraged. With practice your gratitude will flow like a river, and it will show like a river!

Be even more Self-Aware!

Continue the journey of self-awareness. The beauty of self-awareness is it is energy well spent. We can't control other people, but we can control ourselves. Self-awareness keeps us focused on what we *can* change. This awareness will also point us toward ownership. Owning our actions and behaviors, which puts us in a good place to improve relationships. Which improves mental health, which leads to growth. Which leads to more self-awareness.

As you can see, I'm a salesperson for self-awareness! Do you remember when green ketchup was on the market, about twenty years ago? We were dining out one morning and a lady came to our table with a sample of green ketchup. It takes a whole lot of food coloring to turn red catsup green!

She had touched the ketchup and her fingers were stained green. "Oh, would you look at that?" she exclaimed, aware of the mess. What she wasn't aware of is that her tongue was even more of a green mess from tasting it. This struck me as funny because she was sort of judging her green fingers but had no clue about the tongue! Guess you had to be there to appreciate it. Don't be unaware of the parts of yourself you can't see. You can be sure everyone else sees what you can't. There's a sobering thought.

The willingness to examine oneself takes courage a-plenty! Rarely is dopamine there to soothe us, not many accolades and few, *I'm so proud of myself* moments. More than likely, you will be embarrassed and humiliated. As quoted earlier in this book, "If you can't look back to when you were young and say, 'I was an idiot', then you are probably still an idiot". Yes, self-awareness is a *prickly pear*. When you touch it, you will say, "Ouch"!

Personal growth is a hallmark of being self-aware. You can't have one without the other. We live in a *parallel universe*. It's impossible to see your own weaknesses and strengths, your needs and feelings without seeing this in other people.

Share the wealth!

The *Golden Rule* shows up again. How we treat people is important. I believe the *Ego Box/Value Box* illustration has helped me see how and why treating people the way we do is a *Cardinal Rule*. The *how* is treating others with mindfulness, understanding the *Ego Box* and its role in everyone's perspectives and choices. Especially, how our eyes are prone to judge and label this ever evolving and changing, yet fickle container.

The *why* is also to treat others with mindfulness. Understanding the *Value Box* and its role in everyone's perspective and choices. Being accountable for how we approach our fellow peeps, aware of a *Value Box*, inborn to every person. Not easily described or seen with the eye, but keenly felt and understood with the heart and mind.

Whoever and wherever you are, I am totally on your side. You are incredible. The door is open wide to your potential and growth. Your value and worth are without question. Furthermore, you have a gift to give to this world in need of care, and you are most certainly enough.

I hope the *message* from this book has helped *you* to be totally on *your side!*

About the Author.

Rolland Sarver grew up in west/central Illinois. Interests include Psychology, Life Coaching, public speaking and social causes. Rolland considers friends and family to be most important to him. His writing explores your true self-worth and value, compared to how culture, society and your own mind sees (or undermines) this value. *The Value Message* is Rolland's first book.

Made in the USA
Monee, IL
30 July 2023

40163581R00105